Commenti

Academic Writing for G

D0513271

DATE DUE FOR RETURN

Commentary for

Academic Writing for Graduate Students

ESSENTIAL TASKS AND SKILLS

SECOND EDITION

John M. Swales and Christine B. Feak

 MICHIGAN SERIES IN ENGLISH FOR ACADEMIC & PROFESSIONAL PURPOSES

The University of Michigan Press

Copyright © by the University of Michigan 1994, 2004
All rights reserved
Published in the United States of America by
The University of Michigan Press
Manufactured in the United States of America
♾ Printed on acid-free paper

2007   2006   2005   2004   4   3   2   1

A CIP catalog record for this book is available from the British Library.

ISBN 0-472-08857-2

1004649790

Preface

We have called this small companion volume to *Academic Writing for Graduate Students* a "Commentary." As we explained in the introduction to the main text, we view any instructors using *AWG* in class as colleagues or partners in a joint educational enterprise. Indeed, at the close of the commentary, we solicit reactions and suggestions for further change from such instructors. For these reasons, we have rejected the traditional label of "Instructor's Manual" with its implications of rigorous procedures and set methodologies.

Another reason for avoiding the label "Instructor's Manual" has been our concern to produce a main text that can be used by students and researchers as a reference volume. The term *Commentary* suitably covers the answer key aspect and the associated discussion.

This volume contains commentaries on each of the eight units and on Appendix One. The same format has been adopted for each unit.

- First, we summarize the main aims of the unit.

- This section is then followed by a synopsis of activities given in note form. This inventory is broken down into explanations, language foci, and tasks.

- After the synopsis, there are a number of general notes designed to capture the particular character of the unit, to indicate alternative activities, or to anticipate any problems that may arise.

- The final and longest section is entitled *Detailed Commentary* and consists of discussion of the individual tasks and of some other material.

Wherever possible, we have provided "model" or "sample" answers and responses, but we need to emphasize that, in many cases, these are but one of several possible versions.

CBF and JMS

Contents

Unit One

An Approach to Academic Writing

Main Aims

In Unit One users of this volume are:

- presented with the notion of positioning themselves as writers
- presented with an overview of academic writing characteristics

Synopsis of Activities

Explanations

Audience
Purpose and strategy
Organization
Style
Flow
Presentation
Positioning

Language Foci

The Vocabulary Shift
Formal Grammar Style
Linking Words and Phrases
This + Summary Word

Tasks

General Notes

a. This is the introductory unit. It is designed to prepare graduate students strategically and linguistically for their graduate writing careers. As you can see from the first page of the unit, we have singled out six aspects (audience through to positioning) for attention at this juncture.

b. Unit One moves through these six elements in a top-down manner. Moving from the macro to the micro has a number of advantages in our experience. First, it allows the important strategic issues to be presented first. Second, it emphasizes that if the basic strategy is seriously misjudged, then no amount of minor editing will save it. Third, and perhaps most importantly, the top-down approach is likely to contrast with the way students were taught English writing in the last years of high school and the first years of university. Fourth, it enables both you and us to demonstrate that writing involves more than just the production of correct sentences. Fifth, it allows us to introduce early certain simple processes and techniques of textual analysis. This in turn has two consequences. One is that the semi-analytic approach we adopt interfaces well with a student population well known for its analytic strengths. The other is that it can demonstrate that academic writing is itself an academic subject like many others.

c. The unit does not give quite equal attention to all six aspects. More space—and time—has been devoted to style and flow than to the others. Style can be a confusing issue to first-year graduate students, especially if this is their first experience in an English-medium institution. In such a situation they are likely to be bombarded with informal language not only in informal settings but also in lectures and on e-mail (see Appendix Three). No wonder they feel that they receive mixed messages! That is why we have given considerable emphasis to formal style. (If, however, you are teaching in a non-English-medium institution, this problem is less likely to arise and this section of the unit can be gone through more quickly). We have also given special attention to flow. Although the first part of this section (sentence connectors) is likely to be well enough known, the second part, on *this* + summary word, is, in our experience, something of a novelty. Over and above its intrinsic usefulness, this kind of cohesion (described long ago by David Charles as "how to get out of one sentence and into another") can be used by the instructor to demonstrate that he or she is not engaged in a writing course just like any other!

d. Like much of the book, this unit has been designed to be gone through at quite a rapid pace. Most of the texts and tasks are quite short and illustrate basic points. Many of the points made will be made again later, often in somewhat more sophisticated settings. Pace, in our experience, is more important with this population than complete coverage or overlearning. Like all the units in the book, Unit One is a guide; bits can be left out and some of your own bits inserted. In English for Academic Purposes, we believe that it is essential that the instructor control the materials, rather than the reverse. We ourselves do not teach quite all that we have provided here and we each incorporate a few of our own favorite extras. So should you.

e. The first actual writing task in this unit does not occur until Task Thirteen. Of course, if you find yourself in the situation of knowing little about your students' writing ability, you may want to set a homework writing task at the end of the first class. If you feel you need to do this, perhaps you could ask your students to identify and discuss a current controversy in their field.

Detailed Commentary

In the opening diagram (Fig. 1), notice that the arrows go both ways. Although the unit works through the material top-down, movement in either direction is possible at any moment in an actual writing process.

TASK ONE: Considering the audience

Text A is targeting an educated, but not highly specialized, audience, while Text B is directed at experts. Text A provides quite a lot of background material and is careful to avoid too much technical vocabulary. Text B jumps right into the topic and employs quite a lot of technical terminology that most of us are not familiar with. Indeed, Text A was published in *Scientific American* and Text B in the *AIChE Journal.*

If the students need help at the comparison stage, they could be prompted by such things as the amount of background knowledge presumed, sentence complexity, and the use of technical terms.

TASK TWO: Writing a one-sentence definition

Sentence 7 in Text A provides a definition. Most of Text B is a description and could be considered an extended definition.

TASK THREE: Considering strategy

This section takes us right into the heart of strategic considerations in academic writing and thus foreshadows several of the tasks to come in later units. Students may need reminding that this is not Gene's thesis research. It is data that he has acquired; it is not his own that he has painstakingly gathered. In other words, his personal commitment to it is not that great.

It will probably be helpful to explain that a nonprofit provider might be a government or charity hospital, that a for-profit provider might be a private clinic, and that copayments are patient contributions—for example, if a test costs $30, the patient might be expected to pay the first $10. We noticed that even students who had been in the United States for a while were often unfamiliar with the two types of hospitals and the notion of copayment.

Piloting of this activity in a number of our classes shows that a likely majority opinion is to want to include the "problem" element but not place it as such an obvious "downer" right at the end. One of our students suggested this final sentence:

> Although these findings are provisional (since there may be differences in patient age, income, and level of satisfaction in the two systems), they apparently support other studies. . . .

Here are two other student suggestions.

> Despite the fact that the comparison conforms well with other studies, care should be taken in interpreting the results as other variables may affect the findings. For a thorough understanding, the effects of patient income, age, and level of satisfaction with the health-care provider should be considered in the comparison. Even so, the findings are sufficient as a first approximation for the understanding of the problem.

> Despite the fact that patients in the two systems have not been equated for such variables as patient income, age, and level of satisfaction, these results are consistent with many other previous studies which show . . .

Organization: Good- and Bad-News Letters

The letters, we think, are pretty transparent. We chose them because we find that our students often have stories to share about their own experiences here. You might want to ask your students a few questions. Were they asked to have their English re-evaluated? How did they react? At this point you may want to raise the issue of whether there are cultural differences that your class might like to contribute.

There are also many small things that you might like to comment on in the letters, such as the fact that the letters do not say, "Thank you for your application dated . . .," or the verb complementation of "congratulate someone on v-*ing* or look forward to v-*ing*."

TASK FOUR: Labeling the parts of a bad-news letter

Here are our answers to the questions at the end of Task Four. The bad news is often thought to need a preparatory "buffer" statement. Another difference in purpose is that the writer of the good-news letter knows that she has captured the goodwill of Ms. Wong, while the writer of the bad-news letter is worried about the likely reaction of Mr. Lee and so tries to "make amends" with her closing sentence.

Problem-Solution Texts

You may wish to have a short class discussion on other possible solutions—and their viability.

TASK FIVE: Labeling the parts of a problem-solution text

1. Description of a situation: sentences 1–2
2. Identification of a problem: sentences 3–4
3. Description of a solution: sentences 5–6
4. Evaluation of the solution: sentence 7

In such a short text, it's hard to say how serious the problem is. The problem could be very serious, depending on the answers to the indirect question posed in sentence 4. If the general decline in the amphibian population is, in fact, unnatural, then the biologists have reason to be "alarmed." As for the second question, the author believes that this solution is a good one, because it will provide the background information that the scientists need in order to evaluate the situation. The answers to the last two questions are obviously open.

TASK SIX: Analyzing a problem-solution text

1. Generally educated and familiar with the topic, but not highly specialized (e.g., not necessarily urban planners).

2. That the readers have some notion of what an unauthorized settlement is and the kind of amenities they lack; perhaps also

that the readers understand the relationship among the government, policies on housing, and access to basic amenities.

3. To highlight a housing problem in Delhi, which also happens to be a common problem in other countries.

4. The author uses the word *challenge* to introduce the problem.

5. *This effort* refers to the argument that there is a need for governmental policies to address the problem.

6. The author believes that it may help to alleviate some of the housing problems.

7. If the author believed the solution would not work, then some explanation of why it will not work should be included. An alternative solution should also be proposed.

After discussing these questions, you could also discuss the devices used to maintain the flow of ideas. At this point it may also be a good idea to discuss how other texts can be organized: various kinds of reports, résumés, application letters, textbook chapters in students' disciplines, and so on. Are any of these organized according to the other ways given? If not, how are they organized?

Style

We have stressed the need to avoid phrasal verbs, but we are aware that we may have overdone it slightly in the textbook. We are aware, for example, that some phrasal verbs do not have satisfactory formal equivalents (as in "*pick up* a signal," "*take care* of children," "*check out* a piece of equipment"). We are also aware that certain new fields, such as computer science, are distinctive in that they use much less formal vocabulary than older fields. All that said, we believe that strong stress on the Latinate verb stock is the right approach.

TASK SEVEN: Finding a journal article for analysis

Over the years we have come to realize that this task is important in order for the material being covered to seem "real." This task appears several pages into the unit, but you may want to assign it as homework after the first day of class. We encourage students to use the same article for reference throughout our introductory academic writing course, which covers Units One through Four.

Language Focus: The Vocabulary Shift

Verbs

TASK EIGHT: Reducing informality—verbs

1. caused	6. eliminate
2. investigating	7. reached
3. determine	8. maintain
4. developed	9. decreased
5. constitute	10. reviews

TASK NINE: Reducing informality—verbs

Here are some possible alternatives.

1. created/developed
2. encountered/faced
3. raised/introduced
4. appeared/emerged/materialized/surfaced
5. examined/investigated/analyzed/considered

Nouns and Other Parts of Speech

TASK TEN: Choosing the more formal alternative

We think the more formal alternatives are clear. Here are some suggestions for sentences 6–9.

6. intensified
7. have insufficient
8. rarely occur
9. enlarged to facilitate loading and unloading

Language Focus: Formal Grammar Style

You may need to discuss the following issues with your students.

1. Students may need reminding that *cannot* is one word.

2. Explain, if necessary, the differences between *a few / a little* and *few / little*. For example, "I have few dollars" as opposed to "I have a few dollars" (This is dealt with again in Unit Eight.)

5. The role of direct questions in formal academic writing is, admittedly, somewhat obscure. On the whole, we think it helpful to advise students to cut back on any propensity they might have to use direct questions. One problem we have noticed is that our students often pop in a direct question when it is unexpected. While less dramatic, indirect questions may be a better route to go.

6. The midposition rule applies most strongly to single-word adverbs of time, frequency, and manner. (This will be dealt with again in Unit Three.)

7. Students also need to be sensitive to the unique preferences of individual instructors. Students have often asked us about "rules" cited by their instructors, some of which were unknown to us. For example, many of our students have been told to never start a sentence with *however.*

TASK ELEVEN: Analyzing a journal article

Students should be able to identify in their articles many of the elements described in the Language Focus.

TASK TWELVE: Reducing informality

1. This model can be used to analyze the effects of several parameter changes.

2. Coffee prices have fallen for many reasons.

3. The difference between these two approaches to designing underground subway stations can clearly be seen.

4. Recent research has shown that the arms are commonly used for protection during a fall to the ground.

5. To date, no comprehensive study has examined the role of smiling in gaining the initial trust of individuals.

6. Some studies have concluded that bamboo could be more widely used than it is now as a construction material.

7. These special tax laws have been enacted in six midwestern states: Illinois, Indiana, Iowa, Ohio, Michigan, and Minnesota.

8. Little research has been done on the use of oil palm shell as coarse aggregate in the production of concrete.

TASK THIRTEEN: Writing a problem-solution text

This is the first compositional task in the textbook (although you may already have asked for a diagnostic writing task earlier—see General Note e). It is not our purpose here to suggest to you how you might grade it; whether or when you will ask for a second draft; whether or not you will use some set of correcting symbols; whether or not you might want to encourage peer critique or review either before submission or after hand-back; whether you will, in fact, offer a grade; whether this will be subdivided into content and language; or whether you will want to discuss some or all of the writings in class. These, we believe, are all decisions that you need to make in light of your own situation, experience, and preference. However, we would like to point out that the way you grade the first written assignment and how you comment on this set of papers will, almost certainly, send a set of strong signals to your class.

Flow

As we said earlier, this section deals with intersentential connection and transition, or "how to get out of one sentence and into another." Few NNS students are likely to be consistently effective in doing this on entry to a graduate program, even if their TOEFL scores are high.

TASK FOURTEEN: Considering Flow

Passage A is technically correct in terms of grammar accuracy; however, it is clearly lacking. Get the class to explain why passage B is a more "considerate" text for the reader. Note the summary phrase in passage B (i.e., "this transparency").

Language Focus: Linking Words and Phrases

As you know, these words and phrases go by a range of names. At this stage we suggest that you focus on the middle column of Table 1. Here we find the connectors that are particularly associated with written formal academic English. They are, of course, surrounded by controversy. It can be quite easily shown that the best writers of academic English use sentence connectors very sparingly. However, to our mind, it does not at all follow from this that NNS should be discouraged from using them. Admired native speaker (NS) writers have a host of devices for maintaining cohesion, rarely use a word wrongly, or fall into ambiguity, or misjudge their audience. None of these things are true of most students in our classes. For our students, logical connectors can be a powerful aid for clarity.

Here we present an (incomplete) list and a few basic exercises. This is minimal stuff, since practically every EAP writing instructor we know has dealt with this topic in one way or another. Dealing with the middle column of Figure 2 certainly provides an opportunity for (re)teaching the semicolon.

> Birds fly; however, fish swim.

Certainly, the correct use of the semicolon can be seen as yet another indication of a maturing academic style. Indeed, one of the minor aims of this course would be to make sure that students can command appropriate uses of the colon and the semicolon. At this point it might be helpful to point out that sentence connectors are not restricted to the beginning of an independent clause. All of the following are possible.

> . . . ; however, fish swim.

> . . . ; fish, however, swim.

> . . . ; fish swim, however.

Based on present knowledge, the position of words like *however* and *therefore* is very unclear in academic English. This topic is, in fact, taken up again in Units Seven and Eight as well as Appendix Four.

TASK FIFTEEN: Editing for punctuation

[1]Although most major companies provide their employees e-mail accounts as well as Internet access, many of these companies are concerned about potential abuse and monitor their employees' use of these media. [2]In fact, more than 75% of all major corporations report that they monitor their employees' use of e-mail and Internet access, either by spot-checking or constant surveillance. [3]Businesses have many reasons for monitoring e-mail and Internet use; for example, they may be worried about lawsuits arising from sexual harassment

because of mass mailing of offensive jokes. [4]In addition, there may be concerns about productivity. [5]Recent studies have shown that nearly 86% of employees use e-mail and cruise the Web for personal reasons, thus leading many companies to ban unproductive e-mail, such as jokes, and to restrict Web access.

TASK SIXTEEN: Choosing linking words and phrases

A. Sentence 2: For example
    Sentence 4: While/Although
    Sentence 6: First blank: therefore/hence
    　　　　　　 Second blank: thus

B. Sentence 2: First blank: however
    　　　　　　 Second blank: thus
    Sentence 3: while/whereas
    Sentence 4: Although/Even though
    Sentence 6: For example

Language Focus: *this* + Summary Word

As you know, "unsupported" *this* is very common in spoken English and in informal writing, but it is somewhat contraindicated in formal writing. Choosing a summary noun to follow a sentence-initial *this* is an empowering device for writers. It enables them to communicate to the reader how the previous sentence is being interpreted. Here is an example from David Charles, who was a pioneer in this area.

The students said they wanted more tests.	This request surprised the authorities.
	This statement surprised the authorities.
	This demand surprised the authorities.
	This ultimatum surprised the authorities.

In the sample sentences in the textbook, *this understanding* refers to understanding the differences between formal and informal texts; *this situation* refers to the mismatch between the number of applicants to Ph.D. programs and the number of spaces available.

TASK SEVENTEEN: Choosing a summary word

This task is a subtle exercise in summary word management. It is a matter of getting students to see that the word choice is highly strategic.

1. Four of the possible nouns are neutral, while one, *improvement,* is highly evaluative. *Improvement* would seem to belong more to persuasive than to expository rhetoric. Three of the others look like good candidates; *drop* does not, since the time frame is 30 years.

2. The second one is even more difficult. *Increase* seems tame given that the nonstudent population of the town is about 90,000. *Invasion* seems journalistic. *Jump* seems strange since the increase is maintained. *Rise* is OK, but *influx* seems to us to be the perfect term to describe the phenomenon. This is a difficult example, and if the students didn't get this one, that's OK.

3. Clearly, *changes* is insufficiently pointed and uninformative. The other three are all reasonable candidates, but to us the previous sentence seems to point to *improvements* more than *developments* or *advances,* since there is no technical discussion of changes.

TASK EIGHTEEN: Choosing a summary word

1. view
2. finding
3. problem
4. process
5. disruption
6. situation

TASK NINETEEN: Choosing a summary word

Some good answers would be the following.

1. method/approach
2. decrease/improvement
3. conclusion
4. phenomenon
5. trend

TASK TWENTY: *It* vs. *this*

We've included this task because many of our students have difficulty choosing between *this* and *it* when they write. They tend to overuse *it*, in our experience, which often leads to confusion. This is a very challenging exercise.

TASK TWENTY-ONE: Revising

We like to do a fair amount of in-class revising or reformulating, so that students can understand the thinking that underlies our comments. Task Twenty-One also works well as homework.

Some students do nothing more than go through the specific points for revision. Here is one student's draft revision that showed a lot of thought. We cleaned up some minor errors.

> [1]Turkey is located in the Central Anatolian Fault Zone, which lies along the northern part of the country, running from south east to northwest. Nearly each year the country suffers severe earthquakes caused by ruptures in the Fault Zone, which is one of the most active in the world. [4]These earthquakes cause a great deal of damage and many deaths, not only because of the nature of the fault zone, but mainly because many cities and highways have been built on the fault and because the potential danger of this big giant has largely been ignored in regional planning of the country. [7]Some of the most serious damage in recent history occurred in an August 1999 earthquake that affected a two kilometer wide area and caused approximately 20,000 deaths along with millions of dollars physical damage in three cities. [9]In order to lessen the amount of physical damage and loss of life caused by earthquakes, researchers have begun working on some early warning systems to alert citizens about an impending earthquake. [10]Although the warning systems being developed can warn people only as little as 10 seconds before an earthquake, this amount of time may be enough to get people to safety, especially if there is a thorough evacuation plan. [11]As a result, the warning system may help to decrease, at least, the death rates in the earthquakes.

TASK TWENTY-TWO: Editing for grammar errors

The discovery of fossil fuels **has** had a big effect on **the** development of cities. The use of the automobile has become **the** most important element supporting Ø modern society. And, since a few **decades** ago, the finiteness of natural resources **has been** a source of heated controversy. Cities and **their** development will certainly be affected.

A greater focus on accessible public **transportation has been** one change in current urban planning discussions. It **is widely believed** that there will be an effort to redesign cities in order **to** promote the use of public transportation.

TASK TWENTY-THREE: Editing for spelling errors

There is considerable doubt **whether** this solution will be **effective.** The initial reaction **to** the report has not been **complimentary.** In fact, many observers **believe** that collapse of the system is **imminent.**

Positioning

The point of Figure 3 is to show how all of these considerations contribute to positive positioning. Macro considerations, such as audience and purpose, are very important, but without attention to micro characteristics, writing can be less effective.

TASK TWENTY-FOUR: Identifying characteristics helpful for positioning

The last task is designed to refocus students' attention on the broader strategic issues that have provided the underlying rationale for this unit. Although variation is possible, our own responses to the eight statements follow.

1. U

2. This is kind of a gray area; at this stage, we think, on the whole, that it should be discouraged, although we know of cases where it can be highly successful.

3. Certainly, yes, H

4. Certainly, no, U

5. Yes, indeed, H

6. Yes, indeed, H

7. Except when specifically asked to do this, graduate students should refrain from overreliance on personal experience.

8. This should only be done with balance. One should avoid an all-out attack. Always allow for "praise where praise is due." This issue reappears in Units Six, Seven, and Eight.

9. Yes, indeed, H

Unit Two

Writing General-Specific Texts

Main Aims

In Unit Two users of this volume are:

- presented with a fairly common structure in academic writing—general-specific (GS) movement

- presented with an overview of short and extended definitions

- shown how definitions and generalizations can be used to begin a GS text

- led to writing their own GS texts and definitions

Synopsis of Activities

Explanations

Usefulness of GS texts
Writing general statements
Kinds of definition
Overview of sentence definitions
Overview of extended definitions
Introduction to contrastive and comparative definitions

Language Foci

The Language of Defining and Naming
The Grammar of Definitions
Article Use in Definitions
Restrictive Relative Clause Reductions
Prepositions in Restrictive Relative Clauses

Tasks

General Notes

a. Although this unit is entitled "Writing General-Specific Texts," most of it focuses on different kinds of definition, ranging from parenthetical definitions to extended definitions. There is quite a lot of material in this unit, some of which some students may already be familiar with. Because of this, instructors may want to be selective.

b. There are 22 tasks in the unit, many of which focus on text analysis. Our goal here is to encourage students to get into the habit of analyzing texts, not only in class, but outside class as well. We have found that many of our students read only to extract information. It has not occurred to them to read to identify typical grammatical structures, vocabulary, or organization.

Detailed Commentary

We begin by providing, in Task One, an example of a GS text. The important points to notice here, of course, are that GS texts are fairly common and that they have a structure similar to an inverted triangle. They start out broadly, become more specific, and then end with a broad statement (see Fig. 4).

TASK ONE: Analyzing a GS text

1. 1) Meetings tourism and its importance
     a. Size of meetings
     b. Locations of meetings

   2) Importance of meetings tourism in postindustrial urban renewal
     a. Growth in the meetings tourism market in the U.S.
     b. Growth in international conferences
     c. Importance of meetings tourism in comparison to leisure tourism in Europe

One question that may arise at this point is how you get "more specific" in a GS text. In other words how can one best move from the general to the specific? Be prepared!

2. This question usually generates some debate, but here is one possibility. Statement *a* could be a new sentence 7, while the point in Statement *b* could be incorporated into sentence 8 after the citation. Sentence 8 could then be split. The latter part of the sentence, after *making,* could be rewritten as a new sentence 9.

3. Presumably there are other definitions for meetings tourism, and this is the one that the authors have chosen to use.

The "Selling Cities" passage began with a general statement, which also includes a definition, as do many GS texts. This makes for a nice transition to the discussion on generalizations and later definitions.

General Statements

It's probably a good idea to start this section by explaining what a generalization is. It is surprising to us how many students don't really know what we mean by the term *generalization*. However, a few good examples are usually enough to get the point across. This section raises the issue of audience again.

TASK TWO: Deciding when to begin with a generalization or a definition

In set 1 it would be useful to start with sentence *b* for a discussion directed at a highly specialized audience. Sentence *a* would be a more suitable beginning for a nonspecialist audience.

In set 2, sentence *a* could start a more general text on AIDS, while sentence *b* could start a research paper for an informed readership.

For the final set, we would say that sentence *a* is better suited for a nontechnical audience and sentence *b* for a more informed audience. Any discussion that would follow the latter would be narrowly focused on catalyst technology.

Definitions

We cover many types of definition in the remainder of this unit. We start with a look at short, parenthetical definitions and move to the writing of longer, extended definitions. There is quite a lot of material here, and pacing is important so that students don't feel overloaded. One unexpected benefit of this unit, according to many of our students, is that students may begin to recognize definitions as they read material in their own fields.

TASK THREE: Same term, different definitions

Responsibility of the student.

TASK FOUR: Identifying definitional elements

1. In addition to the examination of historical records, a study of the geologic record of past seismic activities, <u>called paleo-seismology</u>, can be used to evaluate the occurrence and size of earthquakes in the region. Geomorphic (<u>surface landform</u>) and

trench studies may reveal the number of past seismic events, slip per event, and timing of the events at a specific fault.

2. It should be noted that cell phones are not necessarily the same as car phones, i.e., devices intended for permanent installation in the vehicle and which may have separate handset/dial units.

3. The uncertainty associated with the energy obtained from other types of nonutility generators (NUGs), i.e., thermal and hydro, is relatively small compared to that associated with wind.

4. Average raw scores on IQ tests have been rising for years (Flynn, 1984, 1987, 1999), by an estimated three IQ points per decade (Neisser, 1998). This rise, known as the Flynn effect, has received much attention, though its exact nature recently was questioned.

5. Phytoremediation is the direct use of living green plants for in situ, or in place, risk reduction for contaminated soil, sediments, and groundwater. (Note the definition within the definition here!)

6. Procrastination refers to deliberately putting off one's intended actions.

7. Tax evasion is defined as intentionally paying fewer taxes than the law requires, as a deliberate act of noncompliance.

8. Software watermarking is a process in which identifying information is embedded into a file, enabling authors to control the distribution of and verify ownership of their digital information. The purpose of software watermarking is to protect the intellectual property that belongs to the author.

9. Road pricing is a transportation control measure that requires motorists to pay directly for using a particular roadway or driving in a particular area. Economists have long advocated road pricing as an efficient and fair way to pay roadway costs and encourage more efficient transportation. Road pricing has three general objectives: revenue generation, a reduction in pollution, and congestion management. One

simple road pricing instrument is area licensing, <u>which</u> <u>requires a motorist to purchase a permit to take a vehicle</u> <u>into a designated urban area during peak traffic hours.</u>

10. Collecting, <u>defined as the process of actively</u>, <u>selectively</u>, <u>and</u> <u>passionately acquiring and possessing things removed from</u> <u>ordinary use and perceived as part of a set of non-identical</u> <u>objects or experiences (Belk 1995)</u>, <u>is an acquisitive,</u> <u>possessive</u>, <u>and materialistic pursuit</u>. (Note the definition within the definition here!)

TASK FIVE: Definitions in actual use

You're on your own here. Students should be able to find some good examples. We would imagine that most of the definitions will occur early in the articles selected, primarily in the introduction.

TASK SIX: Changing from active to passive voice

Dental erosion is a progressive loss of hard dental tissues by a chemical process without bacterial action.

A much less desirable change would be the following, in which dentists are highlighted.

Dentists define dental erosion as a progressive loss of hard dental tissues by a chemical process without bacterial action.

Including the group that uses this definition (i.e., dentists) would likely result in some awkwardness. Similar inclusions of a group for the other two sentences would also be undesirable. Here are our suggestions for the final two sentences.

The shirking model is a variant of the efficiency wage hypothesis.

Dalle de verre, a kind of faceted glass, is a thick, modern cast glass which is used in concrete-set windows.

Ask your students whether they think anything is gained by changing from the passive to the active voice, as might be suggested by the grammar checker in their word-processing program. In the active, the definitions come across as being more generally accepted definitions in the field, in our opinion.

Sentence definitions can be very useful in starting a GS text. We present a number of sentence definition examples and the common underlying structure. These are pretty straightforward. Students seem to have little difficulty with them.

Term	Class	Distinctive Features	Other Member of the Class
sole proprietorship	business	owned and operated by one individual for personal profit	A *partnership* is a business owned by two or more individuals for personal profit.
star	celestial body	shines by itself; source of energy is nuclear fusion occurring in its core	A *comet* is a celestial body of small mass which consists mainly of gases and moves in an elliptical path under the influence of the sun's gravity.
annealing	metalworking process	a material is subjected to elevated temperatures for a period of time to cause structural or electrical changes in its properties.	*Welding* is a metalworking process in which separate pieces of metal are joined together by means of heat to form a continuous metallic bond.
kava	Pacific shrub *(Piper methysticum)*	dried rhizome; roots can be ground, grated, and steeped in water to produce a non-alcoholic drink	(We were unable to find any other members of the class.)

Questions most often arise regarding articles and relative clauses. Article questions can be superficially addressed in the Language Focus. This would also be a good time to look at Appendix One. If students need a lot of work on articles, it would be appropriate to start integrating Appendix One into daily class work. If necessary, offer a brief review of relative clauses. We have found that students are not always familiar with the standard English terms used to discuss grammar.

TASK SEVEN: Choosing articles in definitions

1. Helium is **a** gas with **an** atomic number of 2.

2. El Niño is **a** disruption of **the** ocean-atmosphere system in **the** tropical Pacific, having important consequences for **the** weather worldwide.

3. **A** white dwarf is **a** star that is unusually faint given its extreme temperature.

4. Rice is **a** cereal grain that usually requires **a** subtropical climate and **an** abundance of moisture for growth.

5. Transduction is **a** technique in which genes are inserted into **a** host cell by means of viral infection.

6. In seismology, liquefaction is **a** phenomenon in which **the** soil behaves much like **a** liquid during **an** earthquake.

7. **A** disability is **a** physical or mental impairment that substantially limits one or more major life activities such as seeing, hearing, speaking, walking, breathing, performing manual tasks, learning, caring for oneself, and working.

8. **A** hydrothermal vent is **a** crack in **the** ocean floor that discharges hot (350–400°C), chemically enriched fluids and provides **a** habitat for many creatures that are not found anywhere else in **the** ocean.

Relative Clause Reduction

Some discussion regarding the difference between restrictive and nonrestrictive relatives would be helpful here. A simple comparison of a restrictive and a nonrestrictive can be done with:

My brother, who lives in Chicago, is a doctor. (nonrestrictive)

My brother who lives in Chicago is a doctor. (restrictive)

The second sentence indicates that the speaker/writer has at least one other brother who does not live in Chicago.

There are a lot of examples given. In order to get through quickly, attention should be paid to the grammar point, not to each individual example. It is possible to do Task Eight first and then go back to the examples to see the "rules." This section also works well as homework. Please note that we have not provided an exhaustive discussion of relative clause reduction.

TASK EIGHT: Reducing restrictive relative clauses

1. metal that is often used → metal often used

2. Should not be reduced. (A relative clause with a modal cannot be reduced, because the modal meaning will be lost.)

3. device that is capable of → device capable of

4. roof which is on top of → roof on top of

5. precipitation which results from → precipitation resulting from

6. Cannot be reduced.

7. flute that is pitched an octave higher → flute pitched an octave higher

8. a process that involves the selective transport → a process involving the selective transport

9. Cannot be reduced.

10. a celestial body which has approximately the same mass → a celestial body with approximately the same mass

Sentences 6 and 9 are tricky because, in each case, it is important to look at what is going on in the whole sentence. In each sentence, the relative clause presents or describes a function of the subject. There is a process, not a constant state. The verbs *cause* and *speed up* are related to the process, not to a final state.

TASK NINE: Handling prepositions in restrictive relative clauses

Students find this exercise useful but challenging. Instructors may be asked for more examples. Be prepared.

1. with	6. about
2. in	7. in
3. to	8. to
4. from	9. with
5. in	10. in

Whereby

In our experience, students like this word. They think it sounds so academic. Students could be asked to make up one or two definitions of their own using *whereby*.

Care in Constructing Formal Definitions

This is a good opportunity to discuss the differences between spoken and written English again—to recycle some of the points that were raised in Unit One.

TASK TEN: Choosing an appropriate class word or phrase

This task lets the students struggle with choosing an appropriate class word or phrase. Choosing the class is often easier said than done.

1. a consonant	a speech sound
2. an ellipse	a closed plane, a geometric shape
3. mitosis	a process in living cell division
4. neon	an inert gas
5. a composite	Several possibilities here. An image made up of many images, a material, a collection of data elements
6. a semiconductor	a material with temperature-dependent electrical flow

7. thermal toughening   a process

8. oxidation   a chemical process

9. cancer   a disease

10. privatization   also a process, but in economics or public policy

11. intervention   a well-planned clinical process

12. (one of your own)   students' choice here

Students should be reminded that the only times *when* and *where* are appropriate for a formal definition are when they follow a specific time *(when)* or place *(where),* as in the following examples.

> The Renaissance was a time when . . .

> Antarctica is a place where . . .

TASK ELEVEN: Writing a sentence definition

Definitions may vary, depending on the student's field of study. The term *conductor,* for example is used in physics, engineering, and music. The definitions of a *bridge* in dentistry and in civil engineering will differ.

Extended Definitions

TASK TWELVE: Analysis of an extended definition

1. components and types
2. examples
3. history
4. applications

TASK THIRTEEN: Analysis of an extended definition

1. Sentence 1: General definition
   Sentence 2: Brief history
   Sentence 3: Etymology of the word
   Sentence 4: Impact of craft that fly in three dimensions
   Sentence 5: Importance of computers and GPS
   Sentence 6: Obsolescence of older technology

2. General-specific.

3. Both present and past tenses are used. Present tense is used for general statement of facts (sentences 1, 3, and 5). Past tense is used in sentences 2 and 4 for statements about the past.

4. *We* here refers to people in general (the readers) and does not refer to the authors (as in "We have argued that . . .") *We* may be appropriate. It can be used in academic writing, but students should be encouraged to see how things are done in their own field of study. Participants might like to discuss whether either or both of these different uses are found in their fields. If *we* is not used, an alternative formulation could be

   This history is reflected by the fact that the Latin word for ship is *navis*.

5. Making a connection to Internet navigation may be a challenge. However, it might be possible to add a sentence indicating that the concept of navigation is no longer limited to navigation of the "real world" and has now been extended to cyberspace. This point could conclude the definition.

TASK FOURTEEN: Ordering sentences in an extended definition

This exercise is harder than it looks. It is not absolutely essential to do it, but some students really like it. Some interesting rhetoric discussions can arise about how to order examples *b, e,* and *g.* Students can be encouraged to discuss palindromes in their first language and give examples.

a. 2   e. 5
b. 4   f. 6
c. 7   g. 3
d. 1

TASK FIFTEEN: Revising an extended definition

Here is a response from one student.

Airbags

An automotive airbag is an occupant restraint system that provides protection for an occupant of a vehicle in a crash. Although airbags may seem to be a somewhat recent innovation, rapidly inflating air cushions designed to prevent crash injuries existed for quite some time before being used in automobiles. In fact, the first patent on an inflatable safety device for airplanes was filed during World War II.

The automotive airbag technology that developed between the 1940s and 1960s was quite similar to that of airbags currently in use. However, those early airbags were very difficult to implement and costly. The main concern for design engineers at the time centered on storage and the release of compressed air. First of all, the housing of the system had to be large enough for a gas canister that could keep the gas at high pressure for a long period of time. In addition, the bag itself had to have a special design that would deploy reliably and inflate within 40 milliseconds. The solution to these problems came in early 1970s with the development of small inflators which used hot nitrogen, a harmless gas, instead of air to deploy the bag. This innovation allowed the widespread installation of airbags in vehicles beginning in the 1980s.

Today the National Highway Traffic Safety Administration estimates that airbags have annually saved nearly 1000 lives per year. In the future even more lives will be saved as new airbag technologies are developed. For example, research is currently being done on as many as six different types of airbags that will offer protection in a wider range of accidents beyond front-end and side-impact collisions.

TASK SIXTEEN: Writing an extended definition

It is very challenging for some students to write an extended definition without referring to a source. If students need to use sources, encourage them to use their own words and to provide appropriate citations.

No response given.

Competing, Contrastive, and Comparative Definitions

If time is a problem, the sections on comparative and contrastive definitions could be skipped. However, the sections do raise a few important points regarding organization and the language of contrast or comparison. A discussion of strategies can be useful here. Students should think about what the best strategy for presenting a contrastive or a comparative definition would be—an independent presentation or an integrated presentation? In other words, should you discuss
one term and then discuss the other? Or should you discuss both terms at the same time? Should the definitions be only contrastive or comparative? Or would a combination be best? Of course, there is no single answer here, but it is interesting to discuss the possibilities.

We have made the three-way distinction for the following reasons. When there is ongoing debate as to what a term or concept is, we classify this as *competition*. When the meanings of terms or concepts are agreed upon but can be confused (especially by a layperson), it may be necessary to write a *contrastive definition*. Finally, *comparative definitions* include definitions that may appear to be somewhat similar but in which, on closer examination, we can identify differences. These differences are generally accepted by members of the field.

TASK SEVENTEEN: Same term, different definition

1. Three kinds: dictionary definition for the layperson (sentence 1), definition for experts (sentence 3), and alternative definition for experts (sentence 4). It would be nice to ask the authors this question, but the effect is that readers can see there is a lack of agreement among experts as to what road rage is. Also, we can see how the lay definition differs from the expert definitions.

2. Yes, it begins with a general definition and then narrows down to the more specific characteristics of road rage.

3. Past (sentence 1); present (sentences 2, 5, and 6); present perfect (sentences 3 and 4). The present perfect suggests that the expert definitions are not accepted fact but reasonable. Sentences with modals reveal the writer's level of commitment to the point (sentence 6).

4. "This cultural phenomenon" is road rage.

5. Sentences 2, 4, 5, and 6.

6. They mean that it may be an exaggeration to call road rage a mental disorder.

7. This sentence allows the authors to call the other definitions into question and introduce other definitions.

8. Their own definition, perhaps.

TASK EIGHTEEN: Analysis of a revised contrastive definition

In our experience, the patent/copyright passage on page 75 gives rise to many differences of opinion. Many students think it is just fine the way it is, but many look at it and say they would not be satisfied. They would definitely want to take it apart and put it back together in a very different way. Discussions between these two groups can be quite interesting. Strategy issues are often raised.

Students should be reminded that *the former* and *the latter* can only be used anaphorically—they can only be used to refer to previously stated noun phrases.

TASK NINETEEN: Discussing a concept from different perspectives

The general definition of procrastination is not contrastive. It's a rather straightforward definition. The authors do, however, show a contrast between optimistic and pessimistic procrastinators.

1. There are many aspects of the text that make it seem "academic": the citations, the vocabulary (e.g., *engage in* rather than *do* in sentence 2), and the use of a summary phrase (sentence 4), to name a few.

2. The general definition of procrastination provides a good backdrop against which to discuss the two types of procrastinator.

3. Yes, sentence 7 tells the reader exactly what (and how many types of procrastinator) will be discussed next. (Highlight this as a form of metadiscourse and explain the usefulness of such expressions.)

4. Sentence 3: instead
   Sentences 6 and 10: moreover
   Sentence 11: in contrast
   Sentence 13: nevertheless
   Sentence 15: therefore

5. *This phenomenon* refers to procrastination.

6. There are times when procrastination takes place for good reason.

7. A paragraph break would be appropriate before sentence 7.

8. Writing the references into the sentences would place greater emphasis on the researchers.

9. The authors might summarize the main differences between the two types, discuss the ramifications of each type, and/or discuss the proposal of their paper.

10. It might answer these questions: Are there different kinds of procrastinator? Can the two kinds of procrastinator change their behavior?

11. Psychology

TASK TWENTY: Writing a contrastive definition

No specific answer here. In our classes some students were slightly intimidated by the given topics. Students should be reminded that they can choose something from their own field of study.

TASK TWENTY-ONE: Analyzing a comparative definition

1. Sentences 4, 7, and 10,

2. Present tense. The theories are "timeless." Although they were formulated in the past, they are still widely accepted today.

3. Sentence 5:　　In other words
   Sentence 6:　　therefore,
   Sentence 7:　　on the other hand,
   Sentence 8:　　for example
   Sentence 9:　　In other words
   Sentence 16:　　For instance

The purpose is either for explanation/exemplification or to indicate contrasts among the competing theories.

4. There are a number of possibilities: perhaps a discussion of the writer's own theory of humor in which flaws in the other theories are presented. Perhaps an expansion of one of the theories; most likely an analysis of a humorous situation (play, book, movie, or something else), using each of the competing theories or demonstrating how they do not always work.

5. The text is actually a general review of different theories. It is mostly a GS text, but it doesn't get more and more specific with each sentence. The text reaches a particular level of specificity and then remains at that level. It doesn't provide very specific detail for each of the theories.

6. No. It simply says that modern theories are variations of old ones, and it only specifically mentions superiority theory and incongruity theory. (There is no complicated motive behind this. Chris simply had exhausted all her resources and did not look for modern versions of all the theories.)

7. If Chris expressed a preference, it was not intentional. Note the absence of evaluative language. However, she has a strong preference for incongruity theory. If she had wanted to express a preference, she would have discussed the incongruity theory last, rather than in the middle. Discussing the preferred point of view in final position is a common rhetorical strategy. (See Unit Eight for more one this.)

TASK TWENTY-TWO: Writing a GS text

No specific answer.

Unit Three

Problem, Process, and Solution

Main Aims

In Unit Three users of this volume are:

- presented with an overview of problem-solution texts

- shown how to describe a process

- led to writing their own process analysis and problem-solution text

Synopsis of Activities

Explanations

The structure of problem-solution texts
Procedures and processes
Causes and effects

Language Foci

Midposition Adverbs
Verbs and Agents in the Solution (passive voice and
  change-of-state verbs)
-ing Clauses of Result
Indirect Questions

Tasks

Task One	Analyzing a problem-solution text—"The Role of English in Research and Scholarship"
Task Two	Midposition adverbs
Task Three	"The Role of English in Research and Scholarship" again

General Notes

a. Problem-solution movement is an important underlying structure in academic writing. This structure could prove useful for the writing of critiques (see Unit Six) or research paper introductions (see Unit Eight).

b. We have chosen to include a discussion of process descriptions in this unit rather than to treat them separately. Process descriptions rarely stand alone. In many cases, the parts of a process are in fact the steps required to provide a solution to some problem. In addition, process descriptions are important in writing up methodology for a research paper (see Unit Seven).

c. Problem-solution texts tend to be argumentative and evaluative. When writing such texts, students should ideally make it clear to the reader why the problem is in fact a problem and how the solution is indeed an appropriate solution.

Detailed Commentary

TASK ONE: Analyzing a problem-solution text — "The Role of English in Research and Scholarship"

Users usually find this text very interesting as it may relate to their own situation. Instructors can expect some lively discussion about whether English will remain as the main language of research scholarship. Although this text is a problem-solution passage, it is a very "academic" one. It looks for a solution in terms of getting the correct information, not in terms of solving any "real-world" problem once the facts are known. Quite a number of research texts have this purpose. This passage also provides a good opportunity to discuss the notion of hedging. (Hedging will be introduced more formally in Unit 4.)

1. No answer given.

2. Sentences 1, 4, 10, and 14 are important for the four parts of the text. Most students feel that these are most important. However, we can also note that the major claim or conclusion is given in sentence 13.

3. He states that there is a problem with the databases used in Garfield's study and then provides support for this assertion. Next, he gives a very concrete example of a serious weakness— the inconsistency regarding Arabic-language science journals. This example should raise some doubts with the reader, making it apparent that there is a problem. (Note the general-specific movement in the paragraph.)

4. Considering that this is a very short text, the amount of detail is appropriate. If it were longer, then it would make sense to critique the databases and the methodology used to arrive at the 80% figure. The number of examples is dependent on the length of the text. Certainly one more would be nice. Can you supply one?

5. There are several examples of hedging here, particularly in the second and third paragraphs. But the number of hedges should not be equated with the level of uncertainty. Notice that in the second paragraph, we have hedged generalizations, but in the third there are several unhedged statements of results for

single studies. Nevertheless, overall, the two paragraphs seem similar in terms of the level of conviction.

6. Garfield 1983; Najjar 1988; Throgmartin 1980; Velho and Krige 1984; Warren and Newhill 1978. All but one of these citations are twenty or more years old. Given that changes in language policy are likely to be evolving, the reference list looks rather dated.

7. Users may like to consider issues such as which languages are acceptable in journals or which languages are used for abstracts.

Language Focus: Midposition Adverbs

This subject was briefly mentioned in Unit One, but we felt it was important enough to bring up again. It's not a difficult concept, but it is easily forgotten. One of the best ways to illustrate how midpositioning the adverb makes a big difference is to move the position of the adverb around—from sentence initial to sentence medial to sentence final. The other midposition adverbs can be found in sentences 5, 6, 9, and 10 of the text in Task One.

TASK TWO: Mid-position adverbs

1. The provisions of the law must be *carefully* applied.

2. Part II of this paper *briefly* describes the laws of the U.S. that pertain to agricultural biotechnology.

3. Myopia, which is *usually* referred to as shortsightedness, is a common cause of visual disability throughout the world.

4. This study revealed that American and Japanese thresholds for sweetness and saltiness did not *greatly* differ.

5. Pulsed semiconductor lasers do not *generally* use the broad gain bandwidth to full advantage in the generation of subpicosecond pulses.

6. Environmental managers are *constantly* faced with having to determine the extent of environmental contamination and identifying habitats at risk.

7. The water supply lines must be *periodically* inspected to prevent blockages.

8. Although many elaborations of this model have been developed over the years, all of them have *largely* followed the traditional specification in presupposing that an individual will choose to make a tax report.

TASK THREE: "The Role of English in Research and Scholarship" again

1. Situation: sentence 1
   Problem: sentence 4
   Solution: sentence 7
   Evaluation: sentence 10

   Students might argue that this isn't really a problem-solution text. This text and its earlier version are different from the Delhi text in Unit One, Task Six, which deals with a real problem. But we would argue that the present text focuses on an "academic" problem and that this is just as typical for the research world as are "real" problem-solutions.

2. Paragraph divisions could be made before sentences 4 and 7, but perhaps only a division at 7 would really be necessary.

3. Responsibility of student.

4. The implication is that this was not an actual solution (or, at least, not an accurate one). See the discussion of "scare quotes" in Unit Six.

5. The passage is attempting a strong contrast between the assumptions of the past and the newly acquired knowledge of the present.

6. The argument in both texts is strong, but because the second text builds on (and critiques) the first one, it seems stronger. This debate could be resolved by a larger study that examines a much larger sample of journals from a wider range of disciplines.

7. No specific answer.

TASK FOUR: Analyzing another problem-solution text—
"Clouds and Fog as a Source of Water in Chile"

This problem-solution text is noticeably different from "The Role of English in Research and Scholarship." It is a "classic" problem-solution text in that it is technical in nature and is concerned with the "real world."

1. The situation and the problem are presented in the first paragraph, while in the first sample they spread over two different paragraphs. In contrast to the previous text, the situation requires little explanation—only one sentence is necessary. Also the nature of the problem is clearer here than in the previous text. We can all imagine the seriousness of the problems associated with the lack of fresh water. A one-sentence paragraph is not a good idea, so it makes sense to continue the paragraph with a discussion of the problem.

2. Nets are erected → water droplets of the fog are collected by the nets→water flows from the nets to troughs→water flows through filters into storage tanks→water is chemically treated→water flows to households

3. Present tense is used because this is a repeatable process.

4. *is now being tested, are attached, are trapped, is then piped, is chemically treated.*

5. The progressive is appropriate here because the testing is being done at the time of writing. From the author's perspective, it is in progress and has not been completed. Although the progressive is rare in scientific academic English, it can often be used to describe contemporary change (e.g., "Scholars *are beginning* to change their ideas about . . .") The verb *to be* can indeed be used in the progressive.

6. *now, approximately, when, then, chemically, finally.*

7. Sentence 4: this absence of rainfall
   Sentence 14: this collection system

   Both of these occur in the final sentence of their respective paragraphs. They serve to summarize the main point of the paragraph.

8. There is nothing fancy or elegant here. The solution is "announced": "One interesting solution to this problem is . . ."

9. Students tend to select the following information.

   _✓_ the dimensions of the nets
   _✓_ the trough material
   _✓_ the storage tank materials and dimensions
   _✓_ the brand name of the netting
   _____ where the netting can be purchased
   _✓_ the duration of the fog season
   _____ the method of connecting the mesh to the posts
   _____ a description of the post material
   _____ the time of day the fog comes in
   _✓_ the time needed to construct the system

10. A new paragraph could be added after the description of the process. Adding this paragraph would also necessitate a change in the first sentence of the final paragraph to ensure good flow.

11. The information about cost could be added between sentences 15 and 16.

Language Focus: Verbs and Agents in the Solution

This would be an appropriate time to review, if necessary, the grammar of the passive. A quick review of the passive is important if you want your students to write a process description. We did not include an explanation of the actual grammar in the text—thinking that at this level it would be unnecessary—but rather focused on why this construction can be useful. At this point you may want to discuss the value of grammar checkers. Grammar checkers tend to flag all uses of passive, leading students to think that the use of passive voice is incorrect.

One important point to stress here is the difference between a process description and a set of instructions. The goal is not to provide information so that the reader can duplicate the process. The goal is to explain how something works or is done. (Of course, this may enable someone to complete a task, but this is not the purpose.) You might consider bringing in a set of instructions for the students to rewrite in a process format. Some discussion of modal use in instructions versus process descriptions may also be helpful. Although modals are more commonly used in instructions than in process descriptions, they also occur in the latter.

TASK FIVE: Making sentences more informative

There are no specific answers here. Students may not be able to do all of the sentences. Consider having them choose four or five to work with. Here are a few sample responses.

1. Bacteria found in meat can be killed by a brief but intense period of radiation between butchering and packaging.

2. Possible harmful effects of drugs can be reduced by carrying out carefully designed, large-scale clinical trials.

3. One class of rocks is formed by the gradual accumulation of mineral particles at the bottom of a body of water.

4. Information on political preferences can be obtained by questioning passersby in a busy public area.

5. Cultures are partly preserved by continuing ceremonial and ritualistic traditions—such as those surrounding marriage or the birth of a child—that have helped to define them.

6. Sequences of events at archaeological sites can be established by identifying the distinct layers of an excavation site and cataloging which items were discovered in which layers.

7. Changes in land use can be detected by comparing images taken by satellite over a period of time.

8. The spread of infectious diseases can be controlled by vaccinations and by encouraging frequent hand washing.

Flow of Ideas in a Process Description

The three ambiguous sentences did not seem to be enough to justify a task, but we think the point should be raised.

1. Does the author really mean to say that the liquid was collected for 24 hours? Most of our students suggested placing *then* in front of *kept*.

2. Was the sample both collected and stored in the same sterile container? Once again, most of our students suggested placing *then* before *stored*. See if your students can come up with something besides *then*.

3. Are the consumers in fact selected by telephone? One of our students suggested,

   After being selected, the individuals were interviewed by phone.

TASK SIX: Flow of ideas in a process

We think the difference between the two passages is rather clear. Passage B flows better because of the use of linking words.

TASK SEVEN: Improving the flow of ideas in a process description

1. The oil is skimmed from the surface using a boom *and then* pumped into a tank for recycling.

2. *After being harvested,* the grapes are crushed to release the pulp and seed *and then* fermented for three weeks.

3. *First,* the glass is cut to size *and* inspected to determine if it has any imperfections. *It is then* heated to over 600°C *and* cooled, in a step known as quenching.

4. A vessel taken from the leg is grafted to the aorta and the coronary artery beyond the narrowed area, *thus allowing* blood to flow to the heart muscle.

5. When water from rain or melted snow percolates into the ground through cracks, it is heated by the underlying rocks to temperatures well above the boiling point. The water does not

boil *but, rather,* becomes superheated *and* pressurized, *causing it to eventually burst* out of the ground in an explosive steam eruption.

TASK EIGHT: Active voice in a process description— "Coral Reefs"

1. Situation: sentences 1–2
    Problem: sentences 3 –9
    Solution: sentences 10–11
    Evaluation: sentence 12

    The "problem section" receives the greatest treatment, because the detail is necessary to understand the problem. The nature of the problem (why it is happening) is not transparent, as it is in the "Clouds and Fog" text.

2. Sentence 6: in response
    Sentence 7: thus
    Sentence 8: if

3. Investigations are under way and have not been completed.

4. The agent is unnecessary. Passive voice here helps keep the focus on recovery.

5. If sentence 2 said, "They are the marine equivalents of terrestrial rainforests," we could consider this as accepted fact. As it stands in the original, the authors are being cautious about making such a strong claim.

Natural processes are by their very nature different from those involving human action. It follows, then, that the verb forms will be different also. Students sometimes think that change-of-state verbs are somehow "special." It's enough to say that these are simply verbs that usually take the active because there is a natural agent that generally does not need to be mentioned.

TASK NINE: Writing a process description as part of a problem-solution text

Here is a sample response from a student. We've cleaned up some minor language problems.

Very often people receive serious muscle injuries as a result of automobile crashes. In many cases muscles can eventually heal themselves with minimal medical intervention. However, sometimes surgical grafts of muscles must be made to restore a person's ability to bend their legs or arms. Grafting, while often successful, is not suitable for all types of injuries, particularly when injuries are extensive and there is little muscle suitable for grafting. Researchers have now developed a form of artificial muscle, which in clinical trials has shown promise. The artificial muscle is made of Orlon, a form of artificial silk, using the following process.

First, the Orlon is cooked and then boiled until it turns into a rubbery substance. The boiled substance is poured onto Plexiglas to form a thin film, from which the excess water is vacuumed away. Once the film has dried, it is cut into 2 centimeter wide strips and baked in a 90° oven. After baking the material is ready for use.

Prepared Orlon has a structure similar to that of human muscle fiber and is naturally negatively charged with electricity. When acid is applied to the material, a positive charge is introduced, causing the ions to attract. This attraction contracts the material like a muscle. On the other hand. when a base material is applied, a negative charge is introduced, causing the ions to repel, and the muscle to expand.

This artificial muscle material has restored some limited muscle function in patients with severe injuries. Further research is needed to determine the optimal ways to use this new material and thereby assist patients who currently have little hope of regaining use of their limbs.

Causes and Effects

There are many ways to construct a cause-and-effect statement. The cause-and-effect statements are italicized in the following text.

The databases are those established by the major abstracting and indexing services, such as the ISI indexes and Medline, which are predominantly located in the United States. *As a result, these services have tended to preselect papers that (a) are written in English and (b) originate in the Northern Hemisphere. For these two reasons, it is probable that research in languages other than English is somewhat underrepresented.*

A causal connector is used in the first instance, while a causal phrase is used in the second. In the next example, *when* is used to establish the causal relationship.

> When the cold air from the Pacific Ocean's Humboldt Current mixes with the warm coastal air, a thick, wet fog, called *camanchaca* by the Andes Indians, forms along with clouds.

Language Focus: *-ing* Clauses of Result

We mentioned the *-ing* clause of result in Unit One but now provide much more detail. One common problem with this structure is that students may think that *-ing* clauses of result can be used with all of the causal connectors. It's important to stress that they can only be used with *thus* or *thereby*.

You may want to find instances of *-ing* clauses of result in articles from your own field or ask your students to. Why were the *-ing* clauses of result used rather than a typical sentence connector such as *therefore* or *as a result?*

TASK TEN: Identifying sentences as part of the problem, process, or solution

1. Problem
2. Problem or possibly process
3. Problem or possibly process
4. Solution
5. Process
6. Problem
7. Solution
8. Solution

TASK ELEVEN: Combining sentences using *-ing* clauses of result

1. Sustainable development would require industry to reduce pollution output and resource use, (thus) *stimulating* technical innovation.

2. The researcher supposedly manipulated the data, (thus) *creating* an apparent effect where none existed.

3. The computer viruses infect executable files, (thus) *damaging* the host computer when the executable is run.

4. The plants extract the nickel and zinc from the soil, (thus) *leaving it* uncontaminated.

5. *When* rainfall levels plummeted, a slow, but steady, loss of grasses occurred, (thus) *transforming* the region into a desert.

6. *When* countries sign treaties on the use of "free resources" such as air and ocean fish, serious ownership questions arise, (thus) *causing* difficulties in enforcing any agreement.

For number 6 many students will want to say,

When countries sign treaties on the use of "free resources" such as air and ocean fish, serious ownership questions arise, (thus) *making* it difficult to enforce any agreement.

We suggest challenging them to find a way to avoid using *make*. For example:

When countries sign treaties on the use of "free resources" such as air and ocean fish, serious ownership questions arise, (thus) *causing/giving rise to* difficulties in enforcing any agreement.

TASK TWELVE: Deciding when to use an *-ing* clause of result or other linking word

The following answers seem the most appropriate to us.

1. b
2. c
3. b

TASK THIRTEEN: Analyzing methodology in an article

You're on your own again, but students will certainly find something interesting.

TASK FOURTEEN: Writing an original process description

No answer given

Language Focus: Indirect Questions

Indirect questions can be tricky for both native and nonnative speakers because there is no inversion of subject and verb. This difference between direct and indirect question may eventually disappear, but for now students should be reminded to follow standard word order.

Indirect questions are useful to introduce a problem. As discussed later in Unit Eight, they can also be used to indicate a gap in a particular area of research.

TASK FIFTEEN: Placing the verb *to be* in indirect questions

1. The question remains whether it **is** possible to develop a reliable earthquake warning system.

2. Current studies provide little information on how this policy **is** being implemented in rural areas.

3. We need to know what precautions **are** being taken to prevent the spread of the disease.

4. There is some question as to whether the current crisis can eventually **be** overcome.

5. It has not been determined how these policies **are** likely to affect small businesses.

6. It might also be of interest to investigate to what extent persistence **is** a major factor in graduate student success.

7. Another issue raised by this study is whether and to what extent poverty and climate **are** linked.

8. The process uses the CPU power it needs, depending on what it **is** doing and depending on what other processes **are** running.

9. The research investigated whether time **is** money and found that $V = \{W[(100-t)/100]\}/C$, where V is the value of an hour, W is a person's hourly wage, t is the tax rate, and C is the local cost of living.

10. It is unclear what the optimal level of government debt **is**.

TASK SIXTEEN: Writing up methodology

Students may express some uncertainty as they begin this task. How much can they simply copy from the text? Can they include information that is not presented in the interview? Should the completed task resemble "The Role of English" in Task One or "Clouds and Fog" in Task Four? Some in-class discussion of the interview and how to use it to write a problem-solution text would be very helpful.

TASK SEVENTEEN: Writing an original problem-solution text

No answer given.

Unit Four

Data Commentary

Main Aims

In Unit Four users of this volume are:

- presented with an overview of data commentary (DC)
- presented with the concepts of hedging and qualification
- given suggestions for dealing with "problems"
- led to writing their own DCs

Synopsis of Activities

Explanations

Structure of DCs
Location elements and summary statements
Highlighting statements
Organization of highlighting statements
Concluding a commentary
Dealing with graphs
Dealing with chronological data

Language Foci

Verbs in Indicative and Informative Summaries
Linking *as*-Clauses
Qualifications and Strength of Claim
Qualifying Comparisons
Dealing with "Problems"
Referring to Lines on Graphs
Prepositions of Time

Tasks

Task One   Sorting sentences in terms of strength
                            of claim

Task Two	Analyzing a DC
Task Three	Considering new data
Task Four	Indicative and informative summaries
Task Five	Analyzing a DC in a journal article
Task Six	Choosing prepositions
Task Seven	Expanding a DC
Task Eight	Identifying elements that adjust the strength of claims
Task Nine	Choosing verbs that make the weaker claim
Task Ten	Modifying statements by adding qualifications
Task Eleven	Selecting the best (incomplete) DC and justifying choice
Task Twelve	Writing a full DC
Task Thirteen	Evaluating comments on a DC
Task Fourteen	Improving a DC
Task Fifteen	Analyzing a DC
Task Sixteen	Analyzing a published DC
Task Seventeen	Writing a DC—the test-retest data
Task Eighteen	Completing a student DC
Task Nineteen	Describing a graph
Task Twenty	Re-assembling a scrambled DC
Task Twenty-One	Writing a DC based on material given
Task Twenty-Two	Writing a DC based on own material

General Notes

a. As you can see (Ah, a linking *as*-clause!), there is quite a lot of material in this unit, but in our experience it can be gone through quite quickly. Indeed, it is probably quite important to maintain a good pace. Pick and choose material that suits your students' needs best.

b. One of the problems with textbooks as opposed to an instructor's own "just in time" materials is that textbooks cannot handle highly topical material. There may well be occasions, then, where you might want to use your own data, culled from a recent newspaper or whatever. This is fine as long as you think through the expected writing outcomes, particularly in terms of academic, as opposed to journalistic, commentary.

c. You will notice from the explanation section that there is a bit of specific—and nontransparent—terminology to be gone through. We are always interested in improving the terminology, so any ideas you may have for improvement will be carefully considered.

d. Some of the Language Focus sections in the textbook are somewhat swift, that is, they assume that students already have a good handle on the basic underlying material. Sometimes in the commentary we offer a suggestion or two for further work if you find that your students seem to need it.

e. There are 22 tasks in the unit. These have deliberately been kept short in terms of both amount of writing and amount of time needed for completion. We have done this to maintain pace. Please notice in particular that only Tasks Twelve, Seventeen, and Twenty-Two actually require the writing of a DC. You may well decide that the writing tasks are too few and/or come too late in the unit. If you do decide this, one possibility would be to do Task Seven orally and ask at that juncture for a DC based on either the students' or your data.

f. Note that this unit deals with data commentary. It does not deal with technical commentaries of objects, as when a botanist describes a plant, an art historian a painting, or an anthropologist a cultural artifact. If you have students from such fields, you may want to substitute such technical descriptions for one or two of the tasks. Notice also that we have in the end decided not to include commentaries on responses to individual questions from questionnaires, such as the following example.

Q11. For my career, good English is
very important	37%
quite important	33%
not very important	22%
unimportant	8%

Commentary on this kind of material is very hard to do in a nontedious manner, and we believe including it would more likely hold the students back than help them learn to position themselves. However, if you have a number of students heavily involved in processing survey data (as may happen in political science or public health), you may want to incorporate it. The general principles of data commentary apply—only more so!

g. In our experience students from certain fields (e.g., those in music) will generally not engage in data commentary at any point during their degree programs. They may have quite a lot of difficulty finding a published DC in their field. For these students it may be useful to highlight the many elements in the unit that can be useful beyond the writing of DCs, such as linking *as*-clauses, qualification, and strength of claim.

Detailed Commentary

TASK ONE: Sorting sentences in terms of strength of claim

This is a quick exercise designed to illustrate the key point made in the immediately preceding text. Pair work is a possibility. Our answer would be:

a. 4   d. 3
b. 1   e. 2
c. 5   f. 6

But as we say in the textbook, some disagreement—especially about options *a, d,* and *e*—can be expected.

Types of Data Commentary

We give five possible goals for a DC. You and your class may come up with others. Typically, of course, several of these goals may be combined. The main point to make is that *all* of them involve evaluation; none of them consists simply of description.

TASK TWO: Analyzing a DC

If you start a class with Unit Four, you will probably do this in class on that day. We suggest pair work and reporting back.

Here are our own answers to the questions.

1. The commentary starts in Sentence 3.

2. Sentence 1—definition; sentence 2—statement of problem.

3. Ah, interesting question! In many ways, yes (see Unit Three), but note that the author offers no perfect solution to reducing the number of virus infections, even though she emphasizes the importance of antivirus programs.

4. Lots of possibilities here: the formal vocabulary; the absence of references to people (e.g., "concern over" in sentence 2); the uses of the passive; nonfinite *-ing* clauses; sentence complexity, especially in sentences 4 and 6; and so on.

5. Sentence 5 seems more highlighted than sentence 4.

6. Discuss the implications of the data.

7. This seems very reasonable, given the importance of this mode of infection.

8. This might be the moment to discuss the "rounding" of numbers. Alternative *b* looks a bit flat and alternative *a* possibly a bit enthusiastic (is 87% really "about 90%"?). Also the intensifying *as much as* (and other comparable expressions) can be sold as a useful way of enlivening the text.

TASK THREE: Explaining new data

For those of us who remember a world with no Internet and no e-mail, the early data is self-explanatory. The shift from 1996 to 1997 coincides with the emergence of e-mail attachments.

After Task Three, we suggest moving briskly along until the indicative/informative table in the Language Focus (Table 9). When you get to the parenthetical sentence in the middle of page 118, you may want to point out, for example, that both Japanese (Kojima & Kojima 1978) and Korean disprefer anthropomorphizing structures such as the following.

A thermometer measures temperature.

This paper attempts to show . . .

The graph suggests that . . .

TASK FOUR: Indicative and informative summaries

Table 9 goes well as part of homework.

TABLE 9 Indicative and Informative Verbs

	Indicative	Informative
show	Y	Y
provide	Y	N
give	Y	N
present	Y	N
summarize	Y	N
illustrate	Y	Y
reveal	Y	Y
display	Y	N
demonstrate	Y	Y
indicate	Y	Y
suggest	N	Y

TASK FIVE: Analyzing a DC in a journal article

No specific answer.

Linking *as*-Clauses

You may want to point out that in "as it has been proved" (sentence *a*) *as* equals *since,* but that this is not the case with sentence *b.*

We are not actually sure whether we have got the prepositional usages correct. For example, would you accept "As can be seen from Table 3"? Further help with this would be appreciated.

TASK SIX: Choosing prepositions

1. in
2. by
3. in
4. in
5. in
6. in
7. with . . . of
8. by
9. by
10. in

TASK SEVEN: Expanding a DC

This is a short task and could be done as part of a homework assignment or orally in class. Here is a possibility.

> Table 12 summarizes the strategies used by a sample of
> Japanese scientists when writing up their research in
> English. As can be seen, . . .

Notice that the opening sentence does not simply repeat the exact
words in the table heading but offers a slight expansion. Also do
not forget to point out that later location statements in the same
paragraph are likely to use the definite article and no number: for
example, "The table also shows that . . ."

Qualifications

In our experience, students have a fairly good intuitive sense of
qualifications already, although they probably have not seen them
laid out and consolidated in such semantic terms. The tricky part is
the concept of distance. You may be able to find some transparent
examples or elicit some.

TASK EIGHT: Identifying elements that adjust the strength of claims

A. According to our results. suggest, probably a motivation that
    plays some role, might be particularly important, may well be,
    can lead to.

B. Currently, approximately, may soon change, could greatly
    reduce, may be possible, promising results.

Of the four examples we give to illustrate distance when the data is
"soft," the first and third should present no difficulty. You may find
it helpful to stress the fact that although the second example refers
to experts, its claim is weakened by the use of the word *view*. It's just
a view, an opinion. We believe that the fourth examples hints at
anecdotal and nonsystematic data, but we could be wrong!

TASK NINE: Choosing verbs that make the weaker claim

In our view, the following are the weaker verbs.

1. indicate
2. suggest
3. question
4. support
5. assumed
6. suggest
7. influenced
8. neglected
9. encouraged
10. depict

TASK TEN: Modifying statements by adding qualifications

Too many possibilities abound to merit sample answers. In our experience, this task works best if it is seen as a sort of game. Who can go farthest? This is almost a parody of academic discourse.

TASK ELEVEN: Selecting the best (incomplete) DC and justifying choice

After all the language work leading up to Task Ten, Task Eleven is deliberately more intellectually demanding.

Student A has organized the material by first going *down* the "Girls" column and then down the "Boys" column. Although giving the average is a good idea, dealing with the table this way doesn't quite bring out the contrasts—and the main contrast should be across gender lines.

Student B gets it just about right (we think).

Student C seems to overplay the differences in rank order. However, as we shall shortly see, there may be a (just) motivation for this.

Language Focus: Qualifying Comparisons

In addition to the examples given, you may want to provide additional practice by getting the class to make statements—like the following— about themselves as a group.

> Women comprise about a quarter of this class
>
> There are three times as many students from Asia as there are from Latin America.

Possible completions for the incomplete examples include the following.

a. . . . having an imposed curfew.

b. . . . that their parents had some say in their choice of friends.

c. . . . being required to save some percentage of their self-earned money.

d. . . . that their future educational choices were influenced by their parents.

e. . . . that restrictions were placed on their use of the family car . . .

TASK TWELVE: Writing a full DC

We do not provide a model answer for this task. However, we suggest that you remind the students to read again the sentences immediately before the table in order to get ideas for the opening sentences. As for explanations, the table would seem to suggest that parental restrictions on girls tend to be concerned with their social life, while for boys the concern is more with career and education. Restrictions on girls tend, then, to be focused on the present, but for boys there is also anxiety about the future.

TASK THIRTEEN: Evaluating comments on a DC

This task is somewhat different in that it asks students to evaluate a content instructor's comments (something that students do all the time, of course). It seems to us that none of the comments are really worthless, but students can vary in terms of how they evaluate them. How they evaluate may also depend on the differing expectations of different fields. For what they are worth, here are our own thoughts.

1. This point seems entirely reasonable and well taken. Maybe we need something like "Although differences between the two groups vary in magnitude, the most striking aspect of the data is that across all six divisions, international students complete their degrees more quickly than do domestic students."

2. This may be unfair. The previous sentence seems to show clearly enough that it is a personal speculation.

3. The point is a good one, but it is not clear whether the available data would support its inclusion. Maybe lots of the international students are native speakers or have excellent English. As we are given no data on language background, perhaps it can be left out.

4. It's hard to argue against this. Surely some statement about how to get at the causes of the remarkable findings would be a very suitable conclusion.

Extra Work on Comparisons

At about this point, you may find it desirable or necessary to review the structure of comparisons in written academic English. Here are a few areas that you might want to think of dealing with:

a. *that / those of*

In informal English, we might easily say:

The tensile strength of aluminum is lower than zinc.

or

The tensile strength of aluminum is lower than zinc's.

But in formal written English, students will be expected to write:

The tensile strength of aluminum is lower than that of zinc.

b. Negative comparisons

These tend to be more common in formal writing. Examples follow.

Magnesium does not have as high a density as aluminum.

The United States does not have as developed a social security system as Canada.

c. great, greater, greatest

Students may underuse this adjective in favor of the informally acceptable *large* or *big,* as in the following sentences.

Extremely high temperatures cause the biggest expansions.

The population of Tokyo is considerably bigger than that of New York.

TASK FOURTEEN: Improving a DC

Here is one revision offered by a student.

> Figure 5 shows how long people can survive in water when wearing different kinds of clothing of different levels of insulation. As can be seen, clothing clearly influences survival times. The most effective forms of protection in all water temperatures are wet and dry suits, with dry suits offering the greatest amount of survival time.

TASK FIFTEEN: Analyzing a DC

Task Fifteen could be done in pairs in class or for homework. Here are our own answers.

Sentence	Purpose	Qualifying Expressions
1	Highlighting statement 1	Nearly
2	Highlighting statement 2	Appear
3	Qualified conclusion	Overall, would appear to suggest
4	Unexpected result	somewhat
5	Possible explanation	probably
6	Unsatisfactory data	with some caution
7	Possible further research	would be one possible direction

TASK SIXTEEN: Analyzing a published DC

No answers possible here, but hopefully students will find this exercise useful.

Language Focus: Dealing with "Problems"

This section is designed to increase appropriate phraseology. As far as we can see, the five verb phrases presented at the beginning of the section are interchangeable—at least in these examples.

The grammatical point about the sentences numbered 1–5 is that *may be due to* requires a following noun phrase (hence the use of the dummy-like *the fact that* in sentence 2). We have met considerable differences of opinion about the acceptability of sentence 5. Instructor's choice here.

TASK SEVENTEEN: Writing a DC—the test-retest data

This is a writing task that can be done in several ways. Students could have the choice of writing a standard DC along the lines they have been studying. This would be like a formal report on the discrepancy. Alternatively, they could write an e-mail message to the professor, maybe something like the following.

To: Professor Smith <prof@xyz.edu>
From: Fulani Fulani <fulani@xyz.edu>
Subject: Results of Make-up Exam April 3

Date Sent: February 13, 2004

Professor Smith,

This is my response to your request for an explanation of the poor showing of the students on the above makeup exam (average score of 72 as opposed to 86).

All my fellow TAs agree that the makeup exam was of the same standard of difficulty as the regular test. I also believe that the proctoring arrangements were also normal.

Part of the explanation may lie in the fact that the students took the test at 4 P.M. on Friday directly after several other classes and at the end of a very hard week. It should also be pointed out that it was very hot on that Friday afternoon. The lower average score might also be attributed to the fact that my section contains several international exchange students with weak English, even though this has generally not been an issue.

However, I do need to admit that I did not work through any examples on the board immediately prior to the test. The students were tired and restless and said that they did not want any examples. It is, therefore, possible that this difference may have contributed in some minor degree to the discrepancy.

TASK EIGHTEEN: Completing (blank-filling) a student DC

Here is one way of completing the passage. For some blanks alternatives are clearly possible.

are shown
measured
was chosen
Figure 6
decrease
presumed
underestimates them during the vacant period

> may be due to
> On the other hand,
> observed levels
> may be reduced
> the effects of

Jiyoung could—with advantage— have used hypotheticals (as in the following revision) when she discusses her assumptions and how they might have been wrong.

> . . . because the model assumed that there would be nobody in the building after 6 P.M. and that the air would be fully mixed. In fact, there might have been overtime workers in the building and the ventilation rate might have been reduced.

Did anybody in your class write *might have been reduced* in the space? Give them a prize.

Language Focus: Referring to Lines on Graphs

We think the labeling exercises are transparent enough. You may get somewhat different terms from mathematicians or from biologists. See what you can elicit.

TASK NINETEEN: Describing a graph

1. peak
2. low point
3. remained steady
4. sharp rise
5. decline
6. sharp rise

A. local minimum
B. spike
C. peak
D. kink
E. leveling off

TASK TWENTY: Re-assembling a scrambled DC

This is a challenging exercise. It is much better to have the sentences on separate slips bundled up in envelopes to distribute to groups. Do this if you can. One appropriate order follows.

a.	7	f.	8
b.	2	g.	9
c.	4	h.	3
d.	5	i.	6
e.	1		

This DC is organized in the standard manner.

Location + indicative summary
Highlight 1
Explanation
Highlight 2
Implications of the data

TASK TWENTY-ONE: Writing a DC based on given material

This is quite a tough task to do, perhaps appropriately so at this stage. Suggest to the students that it would be fine for them to guess at or even "invent" possible explanations. You might want to mention possibilities like recession, job markets, government policy, tuition rates, and, perhaps particularly, exchange rates. As we don't have the full story ourselves, we do not offer a possible model answer in this case.

TASK TWENTY-TWO: Writing a DC based on own material

Make sure that the students hand in their data along with their commentary. Otherwise it is hard to evaluate.

Unit Five

Writing Summaries

Main Aims

In Unit Five users of this volume are:

- presented with an overview of summary writing
- reminded of progress to date
- provided opportunities to evaluate summaries
- introduced to the Western concept of plagiarism
- presented with a brief discussion of contrastive summaries
- led to writing their own summaries

Synopsis of Activities

Explanations

Writing an assignment summary
Paraphrasing in the summary process
Plagiarism
Comparative summaries

Language Foci

Identifying the Source in a Summary
Nominal *that*-Clauses
Summary Reminder Phrases
Showing Similarities and Differences

Tasks

Task One	Identifying significant information in a source text
Task Two	Choosing an acceptable summary of details
Task Three	Analyzing a text for summary and identifying the text-type

General Notes

a. This unit marks a break from the type of writing tasks presented in Units One through Four. In this unit, we pay attention to writing with sources. In order to illustrate some of the more important aspects of summarizing, we have mainly used texts from the social sciences. The advantage of doing so is that the texts should be accessible to students; the disadvantage is, of course, that these texts do not allow us to comment on approaches to summary writing in the harder sciences. Even so, we believe that our general discussion in this unit should provide a solid basis for students who may be quite unfamiliar with the conventions of summarizing.

b. We realize that it is not common for graduate students to simply summarize without providing commentary; even so, we have decided to treat summarizing separate from evaluation because writing a good summary is challenging enough without worrying about evaluation. Unit Six, on critiques, builds on the foundation we establish here and deals with various kinds of critique, including book reviews.

c. The material presented here will also be important for Units Seven (Constructing a Research Paper I) and Eight (Constructing a Research Paper II).

d. The focus here is on "public" summaries, that is, summaries that will be read and perhaps be evaluated as part of a course writing assignment. We would suggest that you take time to discuss again the importance of understanding one's audience. Students can easily become frustrated when each individual instructor has his or her own expectations of a student summary and thus in many ways they are "held hostage" to these expectations. For example, some of our students in dentistry are expected to identify their source, briefly summarize methodology, and then list, in order of appearance in the article, key findings, rather than to compose an original, coherent text complete with nice transitions.

e. The first actual writing assignment comes rather late in the unit—Task Twelve. If you want to get a sense of your students' ability to write a summary, you may want to consider assigning a very short summary before Task Twelve. We suggest that you provide the source text. Problem-solution texts work well for such an assignment because students are already familiar with this text type.

Detailed Commentary

TASK ONE: Identifying significant information in a source text

There is no single "answer" here, but information about the conversion and its effect on agriculture and population should be included. Minor details, such as precise percentages, are not so important. Although there is only one sentence on the topic of encroachment, this, too, should probably be highlighted.

TASK TWO: Choosing an acceptable summary of details

Most students pick either 3 or 4. Most recognize 1 as a presentation of details similar to that in the original text. Summary 2 is not much better than 1 in presentation. In 5, it is difficult to see the magnitude of the growth, because we do not how much "30 times" really is.

Summary 5 also does not reveal the significance of the encroachment problem. How much land is being lost? Many students do not like 4 for these same reasons. Again there is no sense of how much growth has really taken place. Moreover, "A small percentage of agricultural land is lost" is an evaluation. A 1–2% annual loss is not small, as one of our students from Egypt explained.

TASK THREE: Analyzing a text for summary and identifying the text-type

Most students agree with the underlined sections and reasons. With a little prompting students will recognize the text as stating a problem (a need to engage in postindustrial regeneration) and a focus on a solution (meetings tourism). Although the text does not closely resemble the problem-solution texts in Unit Two, it provides an opportunity to discuss how recognizing the text-type can help determine which information is important and help ensure a balanced representation of the original (if necessary) when summarizing.

We think it is important to stress that a summary should to some extent reveal the student's understanding of a text. Copying does not demonstrate that anything has been understood.

Paraphrasing is key to writing a good summary. If time allows, consider asking students to paraphrase the fourth sentence of the draft summary. Then see how their paraphrases compare to the one provided.

TASK FOUR: Evaluating comments on a summary

1. Reasonable
2. Reasonable
3. Reasonable
4. Reasonable
5. Reasonable
6. Reasonable
7. Reasonable
8. Reasonable
9. Unreasonable
10. It seems unreasonable to specify that the length of a summary should be some particular proportion of the original. We both were "trained" to follow the one-third rule, but this does not

seem to be useful advice. At times, one sentence is enough; at others, several paragraphs may be necessary. The reason for writing the summary will influence its length. If an instructor specifies a particular length, however, that is another matter.

11. As outsiders to this area of research, it's hard to say. How old is too old when it comes to research? Answers to this question will depend on the area of study.

Language Focus: Identifying the Source in a Summary

The examples here are straightforward. The importance of identifying the main idea is clear. Students generally find Table 18 both interesting and useful.

TASK FIVE: Identifying reporting verbs in a published article

We often ask students to examine two or three articles and bring their results to class. We then compile a new table to reflect all of the different fields represented in our classes.

TASK SIX: Objectivity of reporting verbs

This is how we filled out the table.

TABLE 19   Objectivity of Reporting Verbs

	Objective	Evaluative
describe	X	
recommend (that)	X	
claim (that)		X
assume (that)		X
contend (that)		X
propose (that)	X	
theorize (that)	X	
support	X	
examine	X	

Language Focus: Nominal *that*-Clauses

Here is another opportunity to discuss the differences between spoken and written English. The tendency in spoken English is to drop *that* with verbs that typically are followed by a nominal *that*-clause. The verbs that are followed by a nominal *that*-clause have been marked in Table 19.

TASK SEVEN: Analyzing introductory statements of a summary

1. This statement is not bad, but the *how* should be omitted. Does the sentence really present the main idea? It seems somewhat vague. The focus is on the impact of the irrigation changes on the population and agriculture.

2. This statement is a little awkward. It could be improved by saying something like "In 'Transformation of the Nile River Basin,' Steven Goodman claims, . . ." But is *claims* really the best choice of reporting verb? The information Goodman presents is not likely to be disputed. Perhaps a better choice of verb would be *explain* or *describe.*

3. This statement is awkward as well. *According to* and *suggest* should not be used together in this sentence. If *according to* is used, then the sentence could read, "According to Steven Goodman in 'Transformation of the Nile River Basin,' . . ."

4. *Mention* should not be used as the reporting verb here. This verb suggests that the following information is a minor point. Better choices would be *state, explain,* or *describe.*

5. As one of our students put it, this seems more fitting for a book or movie review. The river has not been transformed in the article. One way to improve this would be to say something like "In 'Transformation of the Nile River Basin,' Steven Goodman states that . . ."

Language Focus: Summary Reminder Phrases

The trick here is knowing when to remind your reader. In a short summary, it is not necessary to remind your reader, but in a longer summary, such phrases can be helpful.

TASK EIGHT: Analyzing reminder statements in a summary

1. This sentence would be fine in spoken English but is too informal for an academic paper. *Says* can be replaced by *states* or *argues*. An alternative to *get rid of* could be *eliminate*.

2. *About* should be deleted. We can *talk about* or *discuss*—but not *discuss about*—something.

3. "In Bradley's article, he" is awkward. A better choice would be to say, "In his article, Bradley also points out . . ." Some of our students also suggested changing *points out* to *notes* or *emphasizes, Looks like* could also be improved. *Seems* or *appears to be* would be reasonable.

4. This one is OK.

5. We cannot say *concludes about*. The sentence could be rewritten, "Bradley concludes by discussing current risks."

TASK NINE: Adding a reminder phrase to a summary

The reminder phrase could be placed right before sentence 9. The text is so short that there are not many possibilities.

TASK TEN: Analyzing a text for summary, identifying the text-type, and choosing an acceptable summary

1. This summary is too short. It would be OK as part of a longer paper—as a form of support.

2. This summary focuses too much on small details which are not that important. The main idea here is that urban planning can play a role in controlling air pollution.

3. This one is about right. The summary maintains its focus on urban planning and pollution.

4. The summary here adds an evaluation at the end. While this is appropriate for a critique, if your purpose is just to summarize, the evaluation should be omitted.

Plagiarism

The North American and Western European views on plagiarism seem strange to many students. Many are shocked to hear that plagiarism is unacceptable. This is not an easy issue to discuss, because there are so many different views as to what plagiarism is. What constitues an instance of plagiarism for one person may not for another. We give some approaches to writing in Task Eleven as springboards for discussion.

TASK ELEVEN: Determining where plagiarism ends and original work begins

John and Chris differ here. While John draws the line after the third statement, Chris is more inclined to draw it after the fourth. Clearly, statement 3 is a gray area. The degree to which a person follows the fourth approach is very important. In discussions of plagiarism, the notion of *intent to deceive* is often raised. This is an interesting point to discuss with a class.

The issue of plagiarism should be treated very carefully. Students should be encouraged to identify and use standard expressions (as we advocate through our focus on skeletal phrases), but they need guidance so that they can begin to see the difference between plagiarism and using common academic expressions. Have your students find the plagiarism policy for your institution. Take some class time to discuss it.

TASK TWELVE: Writing a summary of the "Nile" passage

No specific answer.

TASK THIRTEEN: Writing an original summary

Students often have difficulty finding their own articles. We suggest you have a few on hand in case somebody needs one. Students will want to know what type and length of article is suitable. Textbook passages usually do not work well. Newspaper or popular magazine articles may cause problems because of differences in writing styles.

Comparative Summaries

Students may need to write comparative summaries for a variety of purposes, such as to complete essay exams or research papers. The requirements of this special type of summary may differ from those of a simple summary. A comparative summary may be neither objective nor balanced. Both making inferences and carefully selecting information relevant to the task are important here.

TASK FOURTEEN: Finding an approach to writing a comparative summary

There is no right or wrong approach to organizing a response to each of these questions. However, some approaches may be better for positioning than others. We offer some suggestions from our students.

Approach	*Instructor Expectations*
1. Look at topics that both Alkon and Farley discuss in their articles and then analyze the similarities and differences.	The instructor probably wants to see if the students can identify where the two overlap—where they agree.
Do not just look at Alkon and then look at Farley. Pull out key concepts that each article discusses and then see how they compare.	Perhaps the instructor wants to see if the students can make connections where he/she has not. He/she is testing their analytic skills.
2. Try to see if the two agree or disagree. Then discuss the similarities in detail, followed by the differences.	The instructor is interested in knowing if you can see where the two agree and disagree. It's probably important to write up the analysis with regard to what went on in class (try to relate the discussion to topics brought up in class).
3. This one is pretty complicated. Maybe Kohl and Jaworski's article should be summarized, keeping in mind how different	The instructor probably wants to see if students can take a new article (maybe it's new) and relate it to things already read and

points in the article are connected to various points in the other articles. If Kohl and Jaworski mention point A and so does Juran, then this similarity should be noted in the summary. At the end, the response should try to show the big picture—maybe generalize about the similarities and differences. Don't talk about each author separately. Organize according to ideas.

discussed in class. Students should show they have the basic concepts.

Since the question asks for themes, not specific details, the instructor probably wants to see if the students have a good overall understanding of product and service quality. It's probably important to see how the articles relate to each other with regard to general ideas.

TASK FIFTEEN: Choosing an acceptable comparative summary

We hope most students will prefer the second discussion. The second tries to show the reader both the similarities and differences between Ziv and Wilson. The text is organized according to topic, rather than by author. It also demonstrates that the writer has understood the two original texts reasonably well. The first text simply provides two independent summaries. The reader of this has to figure out on his or her own where the two authors are similar and where they are different. Because of this independent presentation, it does not reveal a very high level of understanding.

TASK SIXTEEN: Writing an original comparative summary

Finding two good articles for comparison may be very difficult. It is not enough for the two articles simply to be on the same topic. The articles chosen must discuss similar issues or subtopics, so that there is a reasonable basis for comparison. Instructors should have a few sets of articles on hand in case students have trouble finding their own texts.

Unit Six:

Writing Critiques

Main Aims

In Unit Six users of this volume are:

- introduced to critiques and their purposes in graduate education
- presented with an overview of book reviews
- given help with important linguistic features of critiques
- given opportunities to develop their critical-reading skills
- led to writing their own critiques
- introduced to reaction papers

Synopsis of Activities

Explanations

The purposes of critiques
Characteristics of a book review
Evaluating an article
Variation in critiques across fields
Unreal conditionals in critiques
Variation in evaluative adjectives across fields
Critical reading
Negative and positive language in critiques
The characteristics of reaction papers

Language Foci

Evaluative Language in Book Reviews
Unreal Conditionals
Evaluative Language Revisited
Beginning the Critique
Inversions (Emphatic Sentences)
Special Verb Agreements
Scare Quotes

Tasks

General Notes

a. This unit follows directly from the previous one on summary writing and, in its closing pages, prepares the way for the final two units. We have assumed, for pedagogic purposes, a simple rhetorical arrangement of summary followed by critique. We know, of course, that it is also possible to incorporate the critical evaluation within the summary. If students wish to attempt this somewhat more difficult strategy in their freewriting tasks, instructors could well express sympathy with these ambitions. This might be particularly the case if students are constructing a critical review of a body of literature.

b. The main texts used for critiquing are all taken from the social sciences. Our experience is that this material is both accessible to and interesting for most class participants.

Detailed Commentary

We trust that the introduction to the unit is self-explanatory. The only additional point we would like to make concerns students who may be asked to critique nontextual objects. In our view, in the fields of art or architecture (etc.) should be encouraged to critique such things. However, there is very little research into such written genres. Instructors might do best by contacting departments for guidance.

We decided to begin the discussion of critiques by focusing on book reviews, although we are well aware that not all students will be required to write them in their fields of study. Nevertheless, they are a useful starting point, especially since they are so widely available—unlike other forms of critique, such as manuscript reviews.

TASK ONE: Checking what students already know about book reviews

This task will help you know what kind of knowledge base you have to build on. Some students will likely be familiar with published book reviews.

1. D. Most students unfamiliar with the genre will likely think that book reviews are largely negative.

2. D. Book reviews do include some form of summary, but not necessarily at the very beginning.

3. A. A good review of a book can actually help an assistant professor get tenure in some fields; a bad one could block it. A review that is simply a "hatchet job" may reflect poorly on the writer.

4. A. Yes, of course. Much time and effort goes into the writing of a book, and the author is hopeful that it will be well received.

5. A. Some professors encourage their doctoral students to do this.

6. A. We and many of our colleagues in other fields regularly read reviews. It's unclear to us whether most members of a field do.

7. A. Yes, cost is often a key point.

8. A. This sometimes happens.

9. A. This greatly depends on both the author and the discipline. Some book reviewers adopt a somewhat less formal style and use idiomatic expressions from speech.

10. A. Generally yes, but some book reviews do contain references. In fact, in our field, incorporating references in book reviews seems to be on the increase. See Task Five in the textbook.

TASK TWO: Analyzing a book review

1. | *Paragraph* | *Purpose* |
|---|---|
| 1 | Introducing the book/clarifying audience |
| 2 | Highlighting the table of contents/offering praise for attention to detail |
| 3 | Highlighting/giving an overview of the layout of the book/revealing limitations |
| 4 | Highlighting content of chapters 1–3/offering praise for chapter 1 |
| 5 | Highlighting content of chapters 4–5/offering praise for writing, but criticism of content coverage |
| 6 | Highlighting content of chapters 6–8/offering praise for content coverage, despite the fact that the topics in these chapters are wide-ranging |
| 7 | Highlighting content of chapters 9–10/offering praise for content coverage |
| 8 | Providing final commentary and positive recommendation, despite limitations |

2. A "mixed bag" is a collection of dissimilar things or an assortment. The term could be a mild criticism of this part of the book.

3.

Paragraph	Sentence	Part of speech	CO/CR
2	"I <u>appreciated</u> its detail"	v.	CO
	"it served as a <u>nice</u> blueprint"	adj.	CO
	"as well as a <u>user-friendly</u> index"	adj.	CO
3	"a number of them contain <u>helpful</u> case studies"	adj.	CO
	"the layout is <u>sound</u>"	adj.	CO
	"the boundaries placed on . . . this topic were <u>too restrictive</u>"	adj.	CR
	"the book is also <u>limited</u> in its emphasis on"	adj.	CR
4	"offers a <u>well-organized</u> introduction"	adj.	CO
	"most readers will find these chapters <u>useful</u>"	adj.	CO
	"I found the section . . . <u>particularly interesting</u>"	adj.	CO
5	"This was a <u>well-written</u> review"	adj.	CO
	"the connection . . . <u>could have received greater coverage</u>"	v./adj.	CR
	"Part II also offers a <u>thorough</u> overview"	adj.	CO
	"the authors' thoroughness <u>distracted</u> from the flow"	v.	CR
6	"The third part is a <u>mixed bag</u> of terminology"	n.	CR
	"I was <u>especially drawn</u> to the chapter"	adv./v.	CO
	"particularly the establishment of <u>clear</u> definitions"	adj.	CO
7	"this was an <u>excellent</u> synthesis"	adj.	CO
	"Both chapters contained <u>informative</u> sections"	adj.	CO
8	"it is written in a manner <u>suitable</u> for"	adj.	CO

Paragraph	*Sentence*	*Part of speech*	*CO/CR*
8	"Aside from its <u>minor limitations</u>"	adj./n.	CR
	"this book is an <u>important contribution</u> to the field"	adj./n.	CO
	"and will likely <u>inspire</u> and <u>educate</u> a multitude of people"	v.	CO

The criticisms appear throughout but seem somewhat more likely to appear at the ends of paragraphs or in the middle followed by a more positive expression that softens the criticism.

4. Given the author's ultimate verdict, the weaknesses do not seem to be particularly major.

5. To some degree, the reviewer's criticism is certainly always specific to particular points in the book, while the praise is often for the book as a whole. But the reviewer does praise specific elements of the book on several occasions.

6. In one instance in paragraph 5, the author uses the conditional tense (i.e., "could have received") to soften his criticism.

7. Information on the book is generally given in the present tense, while the author's impressions are discussed in the past tense.

8. Yes, because the author is discussing his own personal opinions about the book.

9. Yes, the reviewer addresses both the positive and negative points of the book. He explains his criticisms so that they appear to be fair.

10. We all know that no book is perfect. Not all topics can be covered, and biases of the authors will drive content in one direction or another. By pointing out limitations, it's possible to position oneself as being knowledgeable and intelligent. However, fairness should always be your first consideration.

TASK THREE: Analyzing a book review

No specific answer.

TASK FOUR: Writing a book review

Some students may not have a book that they can review. However, they can put their skills to work by evaluating one of the earlier units of this book.

No answer here.

TASK FIVE: Fairness in writing a book review— a look at a review of *AWG*, first edition

Before undertaking the revision of *AWG*, we collected questionnaires from frequent users of the book to see what we should change. There was in fact little agreement on what should be omitted or added to the text, so we essentially left the basic structure and plan of the book as it was. In our opinion, some of Diane's criticisms hold true for the second edition. Her points are reasonable and fair. But we still think that the opening unit should not only be concerned with general audience and general strategy considerations. We are convinced that there is some *early* need to do some interesting language work, especially in order to demonstrate that students are not taking "just your average language course."

TASK SIX: Critically reading an article

1. Applied linguists, sociologists, anthropologists, or other academic group concerned about the language of research publications.

2. Since we have such a short piece, it's hard to say with certainty. At the very least the purpose is to question whether English is as dominant in research publication as has been proposed.

3. Probably this: Is English as dominant a language of research publication as researchers think?

4. The author concludes that it is not clear that English is as dominant as has been proposed.

5. The conclusions are based on previous research. The author should have included more recent research or at least some original research.

6. All of the research cited is old and does not reflect the current situation well. The author would likely need to rethink the conclusion based on current research.

7. The author assumes that *knowing* how much research material is published in which language is critical, but is this as important as the author thinks?

8. No, it's out of date, but a revised version with current data may make a contribution.

TASK SEVEN: Practicing counterfactual conditionals

This is one of the few oral exercises in *AWG* and can be done in only a few minutes.

Language Focus: Evaluative Language

The issue of evaluative language will come up several more times in *AWG,* particularly as we discuss Introductions and Discussions in research papers. Here we just remind users that evaluation can be expressed through different parts of speech.

TASK EIGHT: Evaluating evaluative adjectives

There are no exact or even general answers here (see Table 20 in the text). Our own assessments follow.

++ = very positive   − = negative
 + = positive   − − = very negative
 0 = neutral, uncertain, ambiguous

In this _____ study, Jones and Wang attempt to show that . . .

0 unusual	− limited	0 ambitious	0 modest
− small	− restricted	++ important	− −flawed
+ useful	+ significant	+ innovative	+ interesting
+ careful	0 competent	++ impressive	++ elegant
0 simple	0 traditional	0 complex	0 small-scale
0 exploratory	++ remarkable	0 preliminary	− − unsatisfactory

Evaluative Adjectives across the Disciplines

Note in Table 20 how the adjective "scholarly" is viewed differently in the humanities and social sciences. Note how the three fields characterize poor work: in the humanities it is faulted by a lack of "richness"; in the social sciences by a lack of well-researched data or evidence; and in physics by a lack of attention to detail. Apart from *neat,* how do participants react to *solid* or *painstaking* or *exhaustive?* Would instructors agree with the following characterization of work in EAP?

Good Work	*Average Work*	*Poor Work*
imaginative	competent	superficial
well-researched	useful	prescriptive

Critical Reading

Many of the previous tasks have involved analyses of various kinds of texts. More particularly, Unit Four focused on the critical analysis of data, and the end of Unit Five focused on evaluative comparisons. In this section these skills are brought together in the critical assessment of academic text.

TASK NINE: Evaluating a brief report

1. The main question is whether bullying is prevalent at this particular middle school in Rome, Italy. In their attempt to answer this question, the authors address other questions as well.

2. They conclude that bullying is prevalent.

3. There is room for debate here. It seems to us that the data is not sufficient to make such a strong conclusion, given the authors' reliance on self-report questionnaires and a very broad definition of *bullying.* True, the authors include tests for statistical significance, but the data used for these tests may not be so reliable.

4. The answer here depends on whether you accept the authors' definition of bullying and whether you think the questionnaire data is sound.

5. As you can already tell, we question the broad definition. Such a broad definition would allow almost any unpleasant occurrence at school to be classified as bullying. If the authors had adopted a narrower definition, we would expect the outcome to be different.

6. It is not entirely clear, but we assume they are referring to only those students that had been bullied.

7. No. Table 1 displays only numbers of the students who reported being bullied in the last three months (compare the n of the respondents in this table to the total n mentioned at the beginning of the Methods section). As the Results section states, over half (56.7%) of the students were not bullied in the last three months.

8. The authors have compared their results with those of previous studies. However, the previous studies were discussed in more depth in the introduction, and a direct comparison of results is not exactly done in the Discussion.

9. The authors discuss only one school in Italy, and their results encompass students who were only bullied once or twice, rather than repeatedly. There may also be other types of bullying which were not discussed here.

10. No, this is a brief report. This was not the purpose of the article. However, when a more detailed analysis of the study is published, this might be included.

TASK TEN: Assessing criticisms

There is ample room for disagreement. Indeed, in our experience, students will tend to react to the criticisms according to the standards of their own fields. We note our own reactions here.

1. U. It seems reasonable to assume that the school is typical since it is a public, rather than private, school. The fact that it is in the capital city should not make a difference.

2. R. In our view, this is a reasonable criticism—especially since less than half that number had been bullied.

3. U. While it would undoubtedly have been better to have had balanced groups, we are sympathetic to the likely difficulty in obtaining large, equal-size groups; thus we tend toward U.

4. R. There is other research that links age and bullying.

5. R. Yes, we have said this in our responses to the previous task.

6. R.

Notice the use of *should* + present perfect in comment 3. This structure should be modeled for the class. As for other criticisms, the most common to emerge in our classes is the lack of information from others in the school, such as teachers and administrators.

TASK ELEVEN: Evaluating a critique

There is certainly room for disagreement here. We offer you an analysis from one graduate student.

Sentence	Point	Evaluation	Explanation
4	"and found, <u>unsurprisingly</u>, that bullying exists"	Unfair	The point of the study was not to investigate whether bullying existed, but rather to what extent it existed.
6	"it adds <u>little</u> to our existing knowledge"	Unfair	The results of the study did, in fact, provide results that contrasted with previous studies; even if it had not, it would have added to the existing body of literature on the subject.
7	"As a rather <u>small</u> study"	Fair	
9	"the study has two <u>major limitations</u>"	Fair	
13	"<u>Minimally</u> . . . questionnaire data should have been collected from teachers and administrators."	Fair	

Sentence	Point	Evaluation	Explanation
15	"an even more serious limitation"	Fair	
17	"It is quite unfortunate that Baldry and Farrington have adopted a very broad definition."	Fair	Although the criticism is fair, did the writer have to say "It is quite unfortunate"?
18	"their definition is so broad that it would include everything"	Fair	Here, too, the point is fair, but it could be more diplomatically stated.
19	"fails to consider the importance of the imbalance in the power"	Maybe unfair	Baldry and Farrington take into account the age difference between bully and victim, which is the primary source of the power differential here.
20	"percentages of bullying behavior . . . are too high"	Probably fair	
20	"fail to capture the more serious, ongoing oppression"	Fair	Fair, but *fail* seems very strong.
22	"that the authors did not seriously consider . . . completely undermines"	Unfair	Seems a bit strong. Has the study been undermined?
23	"does not shed much new light"	Unfair	It does shed light on the situation in that school and hence the issue.

TASK TWELVE: Editing a critique to achieve balance and fairness

Here is one response.

According to Smith (1999) bullying in schools has become a serious problem in many countries over the past several decades. As a result, there is growing body of literature on the causes, prevalence, and nature of the victims of bullying. In their interesting study of one middle school in Rome, Baldry and

Farrington add to this literature in their focused examination of bullying in one middle school in Rome, Italy. They administered a questionnaire on bullying to all 238 students in the school and found that bullying behavior is quite prevalent.

Baldry and Farrington's small, but interesting study supports many of the conclusions in Genta et al. (1996). It is one of the few studies to examine an entire school environment, as opposed to one age group across many schools, and thus helps to demonstrate the scope of bullying in one school culture. Unfortunately, this narrow focus could also be considered somewhat of a limitation since the results are not generalizable. If in the future the authors extended their in-depth investigation to include more schools and more students, we can begin to gain a better understanding of bullying behavior in Italy and how this might compare to similar behavior in other countries.

The study has two major limitations, both of which likely affected the results and therefore should be addressed in future research. First, the authors collected self reports of bullying behavior over a 3-month period using a questionnaire. As is well known, self reports are not always reliable (Sudman 1977). The study would have been stronger if observations had also been done to provide another source of data. Since bullying behavior is repeated in successive encounters with another person, the 3-month period may be too short to have an accurate account of the problem in this school. Second, a more serious limitation centers on the definition of bullying employed in the study. Although bullying is widely recognized as a serious problem, there is considerable debate as to what constitutes bullying. Baldry and Farrington have adopted a very broad definition of bullying which would include everything from isolated instances of name calling to the more serious persistent acts intended to hurt another student. Their broad definition also ignores the importance of the imbalance in the power of the aggressor and that of the bullying target. Baldry and Farrington may therefore present percentages of bullying behavior that are too high, while at the same time fail to capture the more serious, ongoing oppression of the individual victim (Smoith et al. 1999). It is the repeated psychological and physical oppression of the less powerful by the more powerful that needs to be identified and understood.

This preliminary study provides further evidence that bullying is a problem in many countries. It would be interesting to build on Baldry and Farrington's work and investigate whether changing the definition of bullying would affect student perceptions of bullying. In future studies the questionnaire data could be augmented by including observations of students to note the frequency, severity, and impact of bullying as well as identify the aggressors and the victims. If observations are not feasible, it would be helpful to also collect data from school administrators and teachers to have as wide a view of the bullying problem as possible.

TASK THIRTEEN: Writing a critique

No specific answer.

Language Focus: Inversions

It may be necessary to stress that these inversions are quite rare and should only be used for strongly highlighted comments.

Language Focus: Special Verb Agreements

If the rules given in this section are followed, you should get these answers in Task Fourteen.

TASK FOURTEEN: Special subject-verb agreement

1. was	4. were
2. were	5. was
3. were	6. were

A small number. . . were . . .

The small number. . . was . . .

Reaction Papers

We have found writing a reaction paper to be common in many graduate courses at the University of Michigan, sometimes in rather unlikely places, such as the School of Dentistry. We recognize that this is an underresearched type of assignment, and we would welcome further information from users of this text.

TASK FIFTEEN: Analyzing two reaction papers

	Reaction A	Reaction B
1. Personal expresions	"in my opinion"	"Since I lived in a very rural area, I went away to boarding school when I was 12."
	"As a former elementary school teacher, I know"	"my reaction to the Baldry and Farrington paper"
	"I think that"	"I think it is likely that"
	"I believe it is important"	"While I recognize that this is a short report"
	"I think there is little doubt"	

2. Essentially general to specific.

3. Text A seems to make good use of personal experience. Sentences 5 and 6 make particularly effective use of the author's experiences as a school teacher. The author of text B does not do much with his personal experience. It provides a backdrop for the discussion but does not seem to influence its direction.

4. It's hard to say whether her emphasis on antibullying policies will be effective. If antibullying policies had been covered in class, then she may simply be parroting what was said, adding nothing new. Even if this topic had not been covered, it does not seem like much of an original contribution in our opinion. Reaction B, however, does add something interesting to think about, namely, the issue of religion and immigrant status. This might very well appeal to an instructor.

5. Reaction A seems more clearly to be a personal response to the issue, not the quality of the research. Reaction B, on the other hand, does address limitations in the method as a main focus. Even so, neither reaction rigorously evaluates the quality of the research, as the critique did.

TASK SIXTEEN: Writing a reaction paper

No response given.

Unit Seven

Constructing a Research Paper I

Main Aims

In Unit Seven users of this volume are:

- introduced to the main kinds of research paper (RP)
- presented with an overview of longer empirical RPs
- shown how to look for disciplinary variation in Methods sections
- shown how to analyze and learn from Methods (M) and Results (R) sections
- led to writing their own drafts of Methods and Results sections

Synopsis of Activities

Explanations

Types of review article
The character of short communications (SCs)
Overview of the RP in IMRD format
Introduction to writing Methods
Disciplinary differences in Methods sections (using a scorecard)
The use of commentary in Results sections
Structuring a Results section

Language Foci

Linking Phrases in Extended Methods
Hyphens in Noun Phrases in Condensed Methods

Tasks

Task One   Examining a review article
Task Two   Analyzing an SC
Task Three   Comparing two SCs

Task Four	Sorting sentences into IMRD categories
Task Five	Analyzing a Methods section
Task Six	Using a scorecard for Methods sections
Task Seven	Deciding on what to include in a Methods section
Task Eight	Writing a Methods section
Task Nine	Analyzing a Results section
Task Ten	Assessing advice on writing up Results
Task Eleven	Searching for commentary elements in your field
Task Twelve A	Critiquing a Results subsection
Task Twelve B	Telling a story from numerical data
Task Thirteen	Producing a Results section

General Notes

a. Units Seven and Eight represent the culmination of *AWG*, since together they provide users with opportunities for constructing RPs on their own (or, if that is not yet appropriate, provide them with useful preparatory activities for such tasks).

b. After some preliminary material, the main focus of Unit Seven falls on the two middle sections of a typical RP: Methods and Results. This decision *not* to start with the Introduction doubtless needs some justification. First, we believe that the Methods and Results are easier to write than the Introduction and Discussion. Second, there is strong evidence that many researchers do not write their Introductions first anyway. Third, in our experience, many graduate students often have the *material* at hand for describing their methods and writing up their results, while they may not have completed the literature review so necessary for the Introduction. So, it still seems the right decision to us.

c. Our original miniproject on sentence connectors has now largely been shifted from Units Seven and Eight to the new Appendix Four. Only the Results section remains in Unit Seven and the Abstract in Unit Eight. In other words, we have paid attention to those instructors who felt that the use of applied linguistics material was overdone in the first edition.

Detailed Commentary

Types of Serial Research Publication

We open the unit by talking about several types of RP, singling out two types for more detailed work: SCs (or brief reports) and longer empirical RPs. This restriction continues in Unit Eight.

TASK ONE: Examining a review article

No answer possible.

TASK TWO: Analyzing an SC

1. We presume that Allen Kurta did most of the writing; as we can see from the references, he has already written several pieces on bats. William Martinus apparently found the rare bat.

2. There appear to be four SCs: Davis; Fujita and Kuntz; Kurta, Schumacher, et al.; and Timm. Two of the other references are to books, and the final two are to longer papers (both coauthored by Kurta himself).

3. Paragraph 1: Status of Eastern Pipistrelle in Michigan

   Paragraph 2: Discovery of a new specimen

   Paragraph 3: Details of the specimen

   Paragraph 4: Why the bat died; behavior of this species in Michigan

   Paragraph 5: Possible reasons for the bats being found where they have been

4. They use the phrase "Herein we report a new county record." This occurs at the end of their opening paragraph. They used the earlier part of the paragraph to establish the rarity of the species in Michigan.

5. Allen Kurta is an expert on bats. (He is also a professor of biology at Eastern Michigan University.)

6. The most obvious place to cut would be paragraph 2, which might be reduced to a couple of sentences.

TASK THREE: Comparing two SCs

No specific answers.

Longer Research Papers

We believe that the opening review of what has been covered so far is self-explanatory. Even so, instructors might want to expand somewhat on the summary "Contributions So Far." In order to do this, you might want to skim forward over the rest of the textbook to see how, for example, general-specific organization can be fitted into Introductions. Note also that at the end of the review we take up once again the matter of "positioning."

Overview of the Research Paper

The overview has three parts: a "shape" diagram of the kind users will now be familiar with (Fig. 10); a brief summary of what each section typically does; and a table dealing with linguistic and rhetorical preferences. As elsewhere, the overview is based as far as possible on research studies known to us. Of course, it is possible to find published research papers that do not follow the tendencies we have outlined, but in discourse analysis one counterexample does not destroy the rule (which is always probabilistic). Exceptions are always interesting, however, and you can welcome opportunities to discuss—and perhaps explain—them.

Finally, a few words of explanation about Table 21. The leftmost column deals with choice of verb form. By "high" we mean that about 50 percent (or more) of all verb forms will be of this type, and by "low" we mean about 20 percent (or less). The other three categories refer to the likely occurrence of references, hedges, and evaluative commentary. In these cases "high," "low," and so on refer to probabilities of usage. For instance, we would expect to find some elements of commentary in Introductions but not so many in Methods.

TASK FOUR: Sorting sentences into IMRD categories

This task is another example of our practice of using material about RPs to illustrate RP writing. While some may find this strategy excessively self-reflexive, it does have a number of advantages. First, the content is equally accessible to all the class. Second, it maintains focus on linguistic and rhetorical levels. Third, the content falls within the instructor's own range of expertise. Finally, it underlines the fact that studying academic writing is itself a valid research area.

The details of the Thompson article are given in the References section of the textbook. The only sentence that is hard to place in a section is sentence 5. If the user bears in mind that there are precisely *two* sentences from each section, its origin can be confirmed by elimination. The correct answers follow.

1. D   5. D
2. M   6. R
3. M   7. I
4. I   8. R

TASK FIVE: Analyzing a Methods section

1. The shortest sentence is sentence 16 (7 words); the longest is sentence 4 (57 words). Quite a difference!

2. The opening sentence.

3. In sentences 2 and 15–17 the author uses plural verbs, thus indicating that she thinks *data* is plural. However, in sentence 1 she uses a singular verb. This confusion is not uncommon; for further information, go to the University of Michigan English Language Institute's Web site www.lsa.umich/eli/micase and look up *kibbitzer* under the MICASE entry.

4. In fact, she went straight on to *(c)*, describing her statistical procedures.

5. There are many options here, but we might choose sentences 4, 9, and 13 so that variation to the use of the passive is spread throughout the text. We also think that these three sentences are quite "interesting" parts of the methodology.

6. Sentence 4: "Prior to the commencement of data collection for the baseline survey, . . . "

   Sentence 9: "After administration of the baseline surveys in 1993, . . . "

   Sentence 11: "In 1995, . . . "

Sentence 12: "In 1996, . . . "

Sentence 13: "In all years, . . . "

Sentence 14: "In all years, . . . "

These are all time-phrases and are used to clarify the rather complex chronology of this project.

7. Here is a possible expansion for sentences 15–17.

> We used the publications of UARC/SPARC users from 1993 to 1996 in order to assess the amount of coauthorship. All the users' publications that were cited in the *Science Citation Index* were entered into a database, along with a full list of coauthors of each paper. Coauthors who were members of SPARC were coded as I (internal), while coauthors who were not members were coded as E (external). Uncertain or ambiguous cases were resolved through e-mail exchanges with the authors concerned.

TASK SIX: Using a scorecard for Methods sections

1. We scored sentences 2–14 at 0 (i.e., neutral). On the one hand, they provided background, had named subsections, used one finite verb per sentence, and had a wide range of linking phrases—earning the passage 4 points. On the other hand, they used the acronym SPARC and had no *how*-statements, definitions, examples, or justifications—causing the passages to lose 4 points.

2. This text is clearly very condensed and receives a score of about -7. The full paper describes a new process (at that time) of extracting proteins from potatoes.

3. Although this text is also from a science paper, it is very different, since it has most of the characteristics of an extended Methods section. We scored it at about +6. The second author told us that they wrote this extended Methods section because the main point of the paper *was* its innovative methodology.

4. No specific answer.

Language Focus: Linking Phrases in Extended Methods

These phrases can be surprisingly common in some disciplines (see Unit Six of *ETRW* for more details). The completion exercise can be done orally by more advanced classes.

Language Focus: Hyphens in Noun Phrases in Condensed Methods

a factory making small cars/a small factory making cars

paper (of unknown color) with blue lines on it/blue paper with lines (of unknown color) on it

personnel paid by the university/personnel at the university in paid employment, but not necessarily paid by the university (could be paid by some outside group)

A light-gray laptop (light in color)/a light gray laptop (one that is gray and light in weight)

artificial-heart valve (a valve in or for an artificial heart)/artificial heart valve (an artificial valve in or for a real heart)

dominant-group member (member of a dominant group)/dominant group member (dominant member of or in a group)

traditional food programs (either standard programs for providing food or programs for providing traditional food)

rapid-release mechanism (a mechanism that produces a rapid [i.e., very quick] release)/rapid release mechanism (a mechanism that releases many times in a short period)

strong-acting director (a director who takes strong actions)/strong acting director (an acting director who is [nevertheless?] strong and decisive or, possibly, a director of actors who is strong)

TASK SEVEN: Deciding on what to include in a Methods section

There are many options here for what might—and might not—be chosen. Here is a fairly neutral or intermediate account.

> This preliminary qualitative study is based on 10 interviews with elderly Chinese living in a midsized town in the U.S. Midwest. The

age of the interviewees ranged from *xx* to *xx* years; *x* were male and *x* female. The interviews were conducted with no other family members present and in the language the interviewees preferred (*x* in Mandarin, *x* in English, and *x* in Taiwanese). In these ways it was hoped that the subjects would feel free to talk about their problems and to communicate their deeper hopes and fears. Each interview was loosely based on a series of prepared questions and lasted about an hour. With the subjects' permission, the interviews were recorded on audiocassette for later analysis.

TASK EIGHT: Writing up your own Methods section

No specific answer.

Results

TASK NINE: Analyzing a Results section

1. Yes, it seems very well placed.

2. Our treatment of numbers in this passage follows the "Rule of Eleven"; that is, numbers one through eleven are written out in words, while higher numbers are expressed as digits. You will notice, however, that this rule does not always extend to numbers placed in parentheses (as in sentence 11), to tables and figures (see "Table 23" in sentence 7), or to numbers that are placed first in a sentence (see "Seventy" in sentence 5). Other systems may apply elsewhere, particularly in the sciences; many science journals use digits throughout, even for the number one. Discussion among the class should bring about the various options.

3. Factual: sentences 1, 2, 3, 7, 13, and 14 (six total); interpretive: sentences 4, 6, 8, 9, 10, 11, and 12 (seven total).

4. There is clearly a difference between paragraphs one and paragraphs two and three. Note that most of the factual sentences occur in paragraph one. The remainder of this section contains considerable commentary.

5. The shortened list looks long enough to us. Sentence 11 isn't a problem, because the actual numbers are given in parentheses.

6. Possibly join sentences 2 and 3, 9 and 10, and 13 and 14.

TASK TEN: Assessing advice on writing up Results

1. The first two take the traditional view that Results should be Results and Discussions should be Discussions. The latter two take the more "rhetorical" position.

2. Closer to Woodford.

3. Your choice, we believe.

Table 24
The most interesting point about Thompson's results is that the top four categories occurred in at least half the papers, while the remaining three were presumably held over until the Discussion. We imply at the end of our discussion that writers who are most *sensitive* to their readers are most likely to want to include commentary in their Results sections.

TASK ELEVEN: Searching for commentary elements in your field

No answers possible, but we would assess our own Results section as falling within Type 3.

The Organization of Results Sections

The first article from the journal (which we also use in Unit Eight) has the results organized by topic, while the second is organized by analytic procedure.

TASK TWELVE A: Critiquing a Results subsection

Here is one possible response.

> This is an attractively presented set of results with a nice balance between the tabulations and with useful quotations from the interview data. However, I thought the general information contained in the final short paragraph might have been better placed at the beginning. While it is true in a literal sense that "most of the children reported using . . . positioning/immobility and asking for pain medication or help from nurses," the figures for these four strategies are in fact only 52 percent. It might have been

better to say that "at least half of the children used these pain relieving methods." I was surprised that there was apparently no breakdown of the results along gender lines.

TASK TWELVE B: Telling a story from numerical data

We would probably opt for all eight points listed, except perhaps for point 4, which seems rather less significant. As there are various options for writing up the Results, we do not "presume" to offer a model. For example, one issue would be how much linkage to geopolitical issues to bring in, such as the fact that Swedish is an official language in Finland or the fact that Finland has had a complex relationship with the Soviet Union over the last century. Another issue would be the decision to handle the commentary by language or by time period.

TASK THIRTEEN: Producing your own Results section

No specific answers.

Unit Eight

Constructing a Research Paper II

Main Aims

In Unit Eight users of this volume are:

- shown how to analyze and learn from Introduction and Discussion sections of research papers

- led to writing their own drafts of Introduction and Discussion sections

- given help with writing titles, Abstracts, and Acknowledgments

Synopsis of Activities

Explanations

The functions and structures of RP Introductions
The create-a-research-space (CARS) model for Introductions
Tense usage in Introductions
Establishing a niche
Alternative types of Move 2
Completing an Introduction
Aims for Discussion sections
Moves in Discussions
Variation in Discussion section openings
More on opening moves in Discussions
Expressing limitations in Discussions
Analysis of titles
Use of colons in titles
Types of Abstracts
Tenses and personal pronouns in Abstracts
The structure of Acknowledgments

Language Foci

Claiming Centrality
Citation and Tense
Negative Openings in Move 2
Tense and Purpose Statements
Levels of Generalization
Expressions of Limitation

Tasks

Task One	Analyzing an Introduction
Task Two	"True" and constructed accounts in Introductions
Task Three	Reconstructing an Introduction
Task Four	Analyzing an Introduction from your field according to the CARS model
Task Five	Reflecting on an opening sentence
Task Six	Analyzing Introduction openings from your field
Task Seven	Assessing theories of citation
Task Eight	Writing a short literature review
Task Nine	Editing a review section
Task Ten	Evaluating "negative" verbs and adjectives
Task Eleven	Analyzing Move 2 of an Introduction
Task Twelve	Classifying and completing Move 3 sentences
Task Thirteen	Analyzing Introduction completions from your field
Task Fourteen	Rewriting a textual outline
Task Fifteen	Analyzing a complete Introduction
Task Sixteen	Writing your own Introduction
Task Seventeen	Classifying Discussion openings from your field
Task Eighteen	Analyzing part of a Discussion
Task Nineteen	Analyzing another part of the same Discussion
Task Twenty	Drafting your own Discussion
Task Twenty-One	Analyzing titles

Task Twenty-Two	Discussing one of your own titles
Task Twenty-Three	Comparing two versions of an Abstract
Task Twenty-Four	Analyzing tense in five Abstracts from your field
Task Twenty-Five	Writing your own Acknowledgments

General Notes

a. Unit Eight is the longest unit in *AWG* and, overall, deals with the most difficult material. As in previous units, the illustrative texts serve two main purposes: They focus attention on matters of language and rhetoric, but, just as importantly, they are designed to help users reflect on their strategic objectives in their own academic writing.

b. Users of the first edition of *AWG* should note that the Introduction and Discussion to our own mini-RP is now placed in Appendix Four. The two versions of the Abstract for the "sentence-connector" paper have, however, been retained in the main text of this unit.

c. As some instructors will recognize, the treatment of Introductions remains largely a pedagogical version of chapter 7 of John's *Genre Analysis: English in Academic and Research Settings* (Cambridge: Cambridge University Press, 1990). In this second edition of *AWG*, we have retained a modified version of the original CARS model as well as the original treatment of tense. While we are aware that subsequent research has complicated the picture presented in *Genre Analysis* somewhat, we hold to the view that "simple" models are more pedagogically useful.

d. Users of the first edition of *AWG* should note that the section of Unit Eight dealing with conference abstracts has been dropped. This topic is now covered in greater depth in Unit Two of *ETRW*.

e. Because Unit Eight is both the longest and the last unit in the book, we have reduced somewhat the amount of detail in the commentary and have been rather more selective in the number of tasks for which we provide specimen answers.

Detailed Commentary

The opening introduction to Introductions is, we hope, largely self-explanatory. We need to emphasize, however, a few points about Table 26. First, *move* is a rhetorical concept, not a linguistic one. As a result, a move can be realized in a phrase or over several sentences. Sometimes moves do coincide with paragraphs, but this is not usually a reliable guide. Second, discourse analysis deals with probabilities, not certainties. In other words, not all RP Introductions will fit the model—and often for good reasons. Finally, in longer Introductions especially, moves will be repeated, as in 1-2-1-2-3.

TASK ONE: Analyzing an Introduction

1. Move 1: sentences 1–7
   Move 2: sentences 8–10
   Move 3: sentences 11–12

2. The obvious paragraph break is between sentences 10 and 11. If it is thought that the opening paragraph is rather too long, it itself could be broken into two sentences: 1–5 and sentences 6–10.

3. The opening sentence looks like Move 1a, while sentence 2 takes the reader into the literature.

4. Indicating a gap.

5. Stating the nature of the present research.

6. one of the greatest/Over the last thirty years/many studies/major exhibition devoted entirely to his art/His best-known pictures/compositional brilliance/deep insight into character

7. In the text, two; in the footnotes, seven.

8. The first three footnotes seem well motivated. In the humanities, the long list of works in footnote *a* would seem "clunky" or heavy if placed in the second sentence. Anybody who knows art history knows that *realism* is a huge topic; John sensibly acknowledges this, but avoids dealing with it, in footnote *b*. Footnote *c* also seems sensible if John isn't going to attempt a small piece of "new" art history himself (which he

isn't). The final footnote, though, might well have made it into the main text, given the main focus of the paper.

TASK TWO: "True" and constructed accounts in Introductions

1 and 2. We do not think the "true" story really belongs in either the Introduction or the Discussion. Doubtless, John's interest in correctly identifying the bird species in the pictures will come out in the main body of the paper.

3. No specific answer.

4. As long as changing the chronology is not designed to be misleading, authors should do what is necessary to create rhetorically effective papers.

TASK THREE: Reconstructing an Introduction

The original order was *j, i, c, f, a, d, h, k, e, g,* and *b.* However, many people prefer the first three sentences to be *j, c,* and *i,* because *c* seems to be an expansion of *j,* while *i* introduces a new element. The original order would have worked better if the first two sentences had been combined, as in "America's population is growing older, and the growing size of America's population of seniors has drawn attention to their economic and social well-being."

TASK FOUR: Analyzing an Introduction from your field according to the CARS model

No specific answer.

TASK FIVE: Reflecting on an opening sentence

See the first part of the Language Focus immediately following in the text.

Language Focus: Claiming Centrality

To claim *centrality* is to state or imply that the research topic is in some way "hot," important, or problematic or has been extensively studied. We can see that Almosnino makes a determined effort to make sure that such a claim is present in his first two sentences. Students can be encouraged to offer further examples.

TASK SIX: Analyzing Introduction openings from your field

Attention here should focus on centrality claims or the lack of them, not on matters of content.

Reviewing the Literature

The simplest answer to the opening question is that without any citations we would be reading not part of a research paper but a popular or journalistic account. But see the following task.

TASK SEVEN: Assessing theories of citation

In our experience, this task indeed generates discussion. Most students opt for all theories making a partial contribution (except, perhaps, for that of Ravetz). Other theories produced can tend toward the "political," as in "you cite the people who you want to work with in the future." A good additional question to consider is whether the uses of citation in English are the same as those in other scholarly languages. We cannot stress enough the comment that follows question 1. The reader of a literature review wants to feel that the writer has organized the material in some logical way (see also *ETRW*, Units Four and Five).

TASK EIGHT: Writing a short literature review

Here is a possible Move 1b for the citation text.

> [5]Two of these theories are widely known and generally accepted. [6]One suggests that the role of citations is to acknowledge the intellectual property of previous authors. [7]This theory, of course, underpins the concept of plagiarism, that is, the unacknowledged use of the ideas/words of others. [8]The other major theory suggests that citations function as a means of recognizing earlier achievements and thus show respect to previous researchers. [9]However, over the last 25 years, several alternative explanations for the use of citations have been proposed. [10]There are, for example, at least two theories that are overtly rhetorical. [11]Gilbert (1977) argues that citations are used to give statements greater

authority, while Swales (1990) suggests that citations often operate to indicate what has not been done, thus creating space for the citing author. [12]In contrast, a sociological explanation is proposed by Bavelas (1978). [13]She argues that using citations enables an author to show that he or she is a member of the target scholarly community. [14]Perhaps the most unusual of all these newer theories is Ravetz' proposal (1971) that citations are an economic exchange system whereby authors "pay" for what they have learned by citing the source of that knowledge.

Language Focus: Citation and Tense

We trust that the extensive discussion of the topic of citation and tense is largely self-explanatory. Instructors may wish to point out how some of these uses do not agree with the "rules" of traditional English grammar. With regard to the final point in this Language Focus, it should be noted that certain fields (and journals) strongly discourage the use of the present tense in the subordinate clause.

TASK NINE: Editing a review section

There are really too many ways of adding variety to sentences 3–7 to provide a sample. The task could even be done in a single Pattern III sentence (especially if the writer is a scientist or an engineer). Here is our own version of such a sentence.

> These include correspondence among scientists[1], news reports in newspapers[2], philosophical essays[3], Boyle's scientific treatises[4], and conversations within the scientific community as to the appropriate character of scientific articles[5].

TASK TEN: Evaluating "negative" verbs and adjectives

We believe the following verbs are—at least in most contexts—strongly negative.

b. disregarded   f. misinterpreted
c. failed to consider   i. overlooked
d. ignored

We believe the following adjectives are definitely negative.

  d. misguided   g. unsatisfactory
  f. unconvincing

TASK ELEVEN: Analyzing Move 2 of an Introduction

1 and 2.

Sentence	Criticism	Rating
6	"suffer from some limitations"	Negative
7	"cannot treat"	Negative
7	"is limited to"	Negative
8	"time consuming and therefore expensive"	Strongly negative
8	"not sufficiently accurate"	Strongly negative
9	"suffer from . . . too many semi-empirical inputs"	Strongly negative
10	"can treat only"	Negative

Quite a list!

3. *However.* Other possibilities would be *nevertheless* and *all the same.*

4. Clearly Almosnino wants to arrange matters in such a way that he finishes with the method he plans to use himself.

5. It is likely to be a Move 3 statement, probably stating that the improvements will allow treatment of *asymmetrical flow cases.*

TASK TWELVE: Classifying and completing Move 3 sentences

This is an easy exercise, so attention should also be focused on the phraseology used. The purposive statements are 1, 4, 5, 9, and 10. The Almosnino sentence is 6.

TASK THIRTEEN: Analyzing Introduction completions from your field

No general answers possible.

TASK FOURTEEN: Rewriting a textual outline

The revision of this text should look like the text by Pierre Martin that precedes it.

TASK FIFTEEN: Analyzing a complete Introduction

1. has increased remarkably/front-page news/on numerous occasions/endemic

2. *Clandestine* means "carried out in secret."

3.

Sentence	*Linking Word or Phrase*	*Function*
3	In fact	Preparing the way for a stronger statement
4	However	Preparing the way for indicating a gap
5	therefore	Confirming the nature of the gap
7	In addition	Introducing a further advantage of using biostatisticians
8	therefore	Drawing a conclusion about the value of biostatisticians

4. The gap is established in sentence 4 and confirmed in sentence 5. Notice the language of negative import: "difficult"/"generally unknown"/"unclear."

5. This indeed is an interesting question. We would argue that it might best be considered as an early placement of Move 3d; that is, it functions to state the value of the research procedure adopted (using biostatisticians). After all, these three sentences could equally well have been placed after sentence 9.

TASK SIXTEEN: Writing your own Introduction

No answer possible

Discussion Sections

We have done our best to offer some general advice for Discussions. However, in Discussions, unlike in Introductions, very much more depends on the exact nature of the results found. Note also that there are no real contradictions in the series of *or*-statements. Discussions, for example, should be both more "theoretical" and more "applied" than Results sections.

TASK SEVENTEEN: Classifying Discussion openings from your field

No specific answer. However, students should be encouraged to use their own classification schemes.

TASK EIGHTEEN: Analyzing part of a Discussion

1. Four (sentences 2, 4, 5, and 7).

2. *Cf.* stands for the Latin *conferre* and now means "compare." It is often deliberately vague, as when authors do not want to detail the exact relationships among items from the previous literature. See Appendix Two in the textbook for more on Latin expressions.

3. The Results are much more detailed, including a table and several individual quotations. The Discussion is more general, relates to the relevant literature, reiterates that "[t]his phenomenon in the children requires specific attention," and goes on to make some practical recommendations. Indeed, it does most of the things mentioned in the series of *or*-statements.

4. They justify why it has been important to "achieve the children's own perspective."

5. Paragraph 2 discusses the pain relieving methods that the children reported using, as well as the guidance given to them by nurses and parents regarding these methods. The third paragraph discusses the different roles played by nurses and parents in relieving pain.

6. Actually it was called "Relevance of the Results to Nursing Practice."

TASK NINETEEN: Analyzing another part of the same Discussion

1. Yes, in a sense. On the local level, it discusses ways of reducing problems with an interview methodology. More generally, it does not deal with the actual problem of reducing children's postoperative pain.

2. Good news → bad news. The opening good news immediately signals achievement, while the bad news indicates sensitivity to problems in the methodology.

3. Sentence 1: *some* defects
   Sentence 2: *some* children *may* have tried
   Sentence 3: problems that *may* have disturbed

4. Here is one of several possibilities.

   For example, some children suffered from severe headaches which impaired their ability to concentrate on the questions.

   In the article itself, we find

   For example, practical issues independent of the researcher included conducting the interviews just prior to the child's discharge, and use of an unfamiliar hospital room as the place for conducting interviews.

5. The first author (1) personally coded and analyzed the data, (2) coded the categories three times at one-month intervals, (3) discussed discrepancies with two independent researchers, and (4) supported her categorization from previous research. How many did you get?

TASK TWENTY: Drafting your own Discussion

No specific answer.

TASK TWENTY-ONE: Analyzing titles

TABLE 29   RP Title Analysis

Title	Number of Words	Any Verbs	Punctuation	Field
1	9	No	Colon	Nursing
2	12	1	Colon	Urban planning
3	8	2	Colon	Marketing
4	11	0	None	Language sciences
5	8	0	None	Language sciences
6	15	1	Colon/ scare quotes	Language sciences
7	11	1?	None	Nursing
8	16?	0	None	Aerospace engineering

The questions arise with whether *hospitalized* could be considered a verb in title 7 and whether *angle-of-attack* is one word or three in title 8.

TASK TWENTY-TWO: Discussing one of your own titles

No specific answer.

TASK TWENTY-THREE: Comparing two versions of an Abstract

1. Both versions qualify.

2. Version A is "results driven," and version B is an "RP summary."

3. Version A uses the past tense except for the concluding sentence; version B uses the present tense except when describing results.

4. Our guess is that generally people in science will prefer version A because it concentrates on the "facts." People in other fields may prefer version B because it explains better why the study was undertaken.

5. sentence connectors, position, academic writing.

TASK TWENTY-FOUR: Analyze tense in five Abstracts from your field

No specific answer.

Acknowledgments

Although we believe that our analysis has merit, we are aware that there is considerable variation from one discipline to another. Users are urged to study standard practices in their own fields.

TASK TWENTY-FIVE: Writing your own Acknowledgments

One form of thanks that you might want to include is to thank somebody for assistance with the English language, perhaps even your instructor. How would you word it?

Appendix One

Articles in Academic Writing

It goes without saying that article use is a problem for many NNSs. In Appendix One, we have not provided an exhaustive discussion of articles but, rather, focused on some key points that can be easily managed within the context of a writing course. As stated in the appendix, a more thorough treatment of articles can be found in Peter Master's research papers. We hope that the explanations and exercises we have provided in the text are reasonably straightforward. To be sure, there is considerable room for supplementation. For example, it might be helpful to bring in some material on article use and place-names.

Since the explanations in the text are reasonably complete (we hope), we have opted here to simply provide answers for the tasks.

TASK ONE

commodity	*C*	money	*U*
complication	*C*	problem	*C*
computer	*C*	progress	*U*
device	*C*	proposal	*C*
discrepancy	*C*	research	*U*
energy	*U*	research project	*C*
equipment	*U*	researcher	*C*
fracture	*C*	society	*C*
information	*U*	theory	*C*
knowledge	*U*	traffic	*U*
machinery	*U*	vegetation	*U*
model	*C*	work	*U*

TASK TWO

This first exercise may be a little tricky. *Writing, reading, copying, thinking, revising,* and *speaking* do not take an article here, because the text refers to all instances of these activities, not a specific instance. The rule of previous or second mention should not be applied. In view of this, instructors may want to consider doing Task Three before Task Two.

___*Ø*___ writing is ___*a*___ complex sociocognitive process involving ___*the*___ construction of ___*Ø*___ recorded messages on ___*Ø*___ paper or some other material and, more recently, on ___*a*___ computer screen. ___*The*___ skills needed to write range from making ___*Ø*___ appropriate graphic marks, through utilizing ___*the*___ resources of ___*a*___ chosen language, to anticipating ___*the*___ reactions of ___*the*___ intended readers. ___*Ø*___ writing as composing needs to be distinguished from ___*the*___ simpler task of ___*Ø*___ copying. ___*Ø*___ writing is slower than ___*the*___ other skills of ___*Ø*___ listening, ___*Ø*___ reading, and ___*Ø*___ speaking. It is further slowed by ___*the*___ processes of ___*Ø*___ thinking, ___*Ø*___ rereading what has been written, and ___*Ø*___ revising. ___*Ø*___ writing is not ___*a*___ natural ability like ___*Ø*___ speaking but has to be acquired through ___*Ø*___ years of ___*Ø*___ training or ___*Ø*___ schooling. Although ___*Ø*___ writing systems have been in existence for about 5,000 years, even today, only ___*a*___ minority of ___*the*___ world's population knows how to write.

TASK THREE

As ___*the*___ average population of ___*the*___ United States has increased, so too has ___*the*___ number of ___*Ø*___ hearing impaired individuals. Approximately __*Ø*__ 20 million hearing aids are now in use, and this number is expected to rise. Although there have been __*Ø*__ considerable advances in __*Ø*__ hearing aid technology, they still have __*a*__ number of __*Ø*__ drawbacks, one of __*the*__ most notable ones being problems in dealing with __*Ø*__ important environmental sounds. For example, __*Ø*__ people who are deaf in both ears are unable to determine __*the*__ direction of __*a*__ sound with __*a*__ conventional hearing aid. This limitation could result in __*an*__ accident or injury if __*the*__ wearer cannot decide __*the*__ direction of __*a*__ siren or __*Ø*__ other warning sound. __*Ø*__ another problem concerns __*Ø*__ people suffering from __*Ø*__ high-frequency hearing loss. This type of __*Ø*__ hearing loss removes many consonants and other useful environmental noises, such as __*the*__ ringing of __*a*__ telephone.

TASK FOUR

To overcome these limitations, researchers have been investigating *the*^ possibility of *a*^ multiprogrammable hearing device that could perform two functions. One would be to convert high-frequency information to low frequencies that fall in *the*^ range of normal hearing. *The*^ other would involve producing *an*^ LED display that could indicate *the*^ probable direction of *a*^ sound. Since *the*^ same device can perform two functions, it could be used by *a*^ wider range of consumers than conventional devices. Prototypes of *the*^ device are currently being tested. If successful, it should be commercially available within *the*^ next five years.

TASK FIVE

Much has been learned about __the__ brain in __the__ last 150 years. __The__ brain, __the__ most complicated organ of __the__ body, contains __Ø__ ten billion nerve cells and is divided into __Ø__ two cerebral hemispheres—one on __the__ right and one on __the__ left. Interestingly, __the__ left hemisphere controls __Ø__ movements on __the__ right side of __the__ body, while __the__ right hemisphere controls __Ø__ movements on __the__ left.

__Ø__ researchers also know that __Ø__ specific abilities and behaviors are localized; in __Ø__ other words, they are controlled by __Ø__ specific areas of __the__ brain. __Ø__ language, it seems, is highly localized in __the__ left hemisphere. In __the__ 1860s Dr. Paul Broca discovered that __Ø__ damage to __the__ front left part of __the__ brain resulted in __Ø__ telegraphic speech similar to that of young children. Soon thereafter, Karl Wernicke found that __Ø__ damage to __the__ back left part of __the__ brain resulted in __Ø__ speech with __Ø__ little semantic meaning. These two regions in __the__ brain are now referred to as __Ø__ Broca's area and __Ø__ Wernicke's area.

Although there is some debate surrounding __the__ specialization of __the__ brain, __Ø__ researchers generally agree that __Ø__ speech is controlled by __the__ left side. There is no debate that in __the__ great majority of cases, __Ø__ injuries to __the__ left side nearly always have __an__ impact on __Ø__ speech.

Final Observations

We have now completed the commentaries on the eight units and Appendix One of *Academic Writing for Graduate Students,* second edition. We have tried to make them open, friendly, and helpful both for instructors and for nonnative speakers using *AWG* as a reference manual or self-study guide. Like the first edition, this book remains a work in progress, and your comments on any aspect of either the textbook or the commentary are always welcome. We can be most easily contacted at <u>cfeak@umich.edu</u> or <u>jmswales@umich.edu.</u>